WHAT MAKES WINNERS WIN

WHAT MAKES WINNERS WIN

Thoughts and Reflections From Successful Athletes

Written and Compiled by
Charlie Jones

A Birch Lane Press Book
Published by Carol Publishing Group

Carol Publishing Group Edition, 1998

A Birch Lane Press Book
Published by Carol Publishing Group
Birch Lane Press is a registered trademark of Carol Communications, Inc.

Editorial, sales and distribution, rights and permissions inquiries should be addressed to Carol Publishing Group, 120 Enterprise Avenue, Secaucus, N.J. 07094

In Canada: Canadian Manda Group, One Atlantic Avenue, Suite 105, Toronto, Ontario M6K 3E7

Carol Publishing Group books may be purchased in bulk at special discounts for sales promotions, fund-raising, or educational purposes. Special editions can be created to specifications. For details, contact Special Sales Department, Carol Publishing Group, 120 Enterprise Avenue, Secaucus, N.J. 07094

Manufactured in the United States of America
ISBN 1-55972-399-8

10 9 8 7 6 5 4 3

The Cataloging-in-Publication Data for this title is available from the Library of Congress.

To my legatees
Morgan, Parker, and Charlotte,
and to their special grandmother

Contents

*"There are forward passes,
and forward march,
and forward thinkers,
and 'Forward, Sons of France,
the day of glory has come'—
but this little thing at the start of a book
is a FOREWORD."*

FRANK DEFORD

Frank Deford

Foreword

To me, the most nonsensical remark in sports is that "the best team didn't win."

Listen, the best team always wins; otherwise, there is no point keeping score.

To be sure, oftentimes the team with the most talent doesn't win. The team with the more famous players (sometimes referred to as "the best team on paper") can lose. The team that should be better, could be better, was better, is usually better, and was favored by the oddsmakers, also often loses.

But from the time a game starts until the final whistle blows, the best team always wins. Also: the best horse wins the race, the best golfer wins the tournament, and the best boxer wins the fight.

The trouble is, nobody really knows what makes a winner. Red Auerbach used to draft somewhat lesser players from winning college programs on the theory that they had somehow learned how to win and could infect the Celtics with this happy disease. The Auerbachian theory was genius for exactly as long as Bill Russell played on the team.

But just as Auerbach was convinced that winning was a spirit that could be transferred, so have I heard many ath-

letes from losing teams promise that the negative experience would make them better winners if ever they got the
chance. Or, phrased in a slightly different way, there are
those who will swear that the need to win is ingrained,
while others maintain that winning has nothing at all to do
with winning; rather, it is the fear of defeat that drives us
toward victory.

Likewise, from winners themselves I have heard: 1) the
really hard part is gaining that first title, or 2) the most difficult part about winning is repeating, winning again.
(Sometimes, in fact, I may have heard those conflicting
truths from the exact same winners, at different times.)

As well, it is my own observation that nice guys don't
necessarily finish last. I have met just as many angels as
devils on the victory stand. And I have met some incredibly
stupid coaches who have beaten some demonstrably brilliant coaches.

Also, trust me: Momentum is absolutely crucial to winning . . . for as long as your jump shot is working, as long as
your first serve goes in, and as long as your fight manager
keeps finding tomato cans for you to knock out. Otherwise,
momentum is yesterday's newspaper.

The fact is, that after three decades of being around the
best athletes in the world, I have no real fix on what makes
winners win. And that's what makes Charlie Jones's book so
telling and true. It shows, with its variety and eclecticism,
and its wit and irony, how the face of triumph remains so
obvious right up to the moment when the next game or the
next tournament or the next season is played.

FRANK DEFORD, bestselling author, *Newsweek* sports
columnist, commentator for Public Radio, and corre-
spondent for HBO's *Real Sports*

Acknowledgments

If you spend any time at all watching sports on television, then you know that in athletics expressions of acknowledgment take on a very physical form.

With that in mind:

Here's a *high five* to Lamar Hunt who took a gamble on me in 1960 when he brought me to the Dallas Texans and the American Football League.

Another high five to Chet Simmons of ABC-NBC-and ESPN fame for taking me to the next level.

An *inside-out high five* to Roone Arledge who showed me what sports television could really be like.

A *forearm shiver* to Jim McKay who took the time to include me in "ABC's Wide World of Sports" family and for introducing me to the creative world of the voice-over.

A *head-butt* to Don Ohlmeyer who instilled in me his personal Olympic challenge.

A *chest-butt* to Dick Ebersol for gathering the rights to most of the major sports events throughout the world, enabling us to have so much fun at NBC.

A *finger point* to Frank Deford, my mentor, who didn't laugh when I told him I wanted to write a book. He then guided me through the entire process.

A *double finger point* to my personal assistant Cheryl Sedgwick who made sense out of my scribbling and dictation.

A *reverse high five* to my creative friends Michael Loftus, Jim Millard, and Kim Doren who shaped my efforts so this really looked and read like a book.

A *hip bump* to Mike Lewis, my editor, who pulled it all together. (Mike moonlights as a clown, which naturally qualifies him to work with me.)

A *double elbow-knock* to my agent Margret McBride who, in reality, made it all happen.

And a final *end zone dance* to the thousands of athletes and coaches throughout the world whom I have met, visited, and broadcast with over the past five decades. There's no question they are truly the ones who made my journey so much fun.

WHAT MAKES WINNERS WIN

PROLOGUE

I grew up in Fort Smith, Arkansas, which in the 1930s was a town of about 24,000. The summers there were always very hot and humid; this of course was before air conditioning had been invented, and like most everybody in town, we had a screened-in sleeping porch so at night we might have some cooling breezes to help us sleep.

My brother Ira and I had a crystal set. Now, you may not even know what a crystal set is. Well, it's a very rudimentary radio. It had a small crystal and this ancient headset with little bitty, tinny earphones. We ran an antenna from the corner of the sleeping porch to the tree in the backyard over to the top of the garage and back to the other corner of the porch.

Then, if it worked right, we would stick a pin into the crystal and we could pick up the 50,000-watt clear channel radio stations around the country. KDKA in Pittsburgh, WWL in New Orleans, WGN in Chicago.

Late at night I would lie awake on that sleeping porch and listen to these "voices in the night" from faraway places. For as long as I can remember that's what I wanted to be. I wanted to be one of those "voices in the night."

There was a Saturday night announcer in Chicago on WGN to whom I would always listen. He came on the air at midnight with, "Hello, everybody, and welcome to the beautiful Aragon Ballroom on the near north side of downtown Chicago. Tonight we feature the musical artistry of Benny Goodman and his orchestra." Oh, I wanted to be like him.

When I turned fifteen my voice changed, so I thought maybe I really had a chance to be one of those "voices in the night." That summer I went down to the local 250-watt radio station in Fort Smith to apply for a summer job as an announcer.

I'd never applied for a job; I didn't know how to go about doing it, but when you're young and you don't know any better you just walk up the stairs, knock on the door, and ask.

When I went into the station, there was a man sitting at the reception desk. In the movies I'd seen, when one applied for a job, there was always a woman at the desk. I wasn't programmed for this. The man said, "What do you want?" and I said very quickly, "My name is Charlie Jones, and I'd like a summer job as a radio announcer," expecting him full well to say they didn't have anything, and I'd be out of there.

Instead, he said, "Come with me."

We walked down a hallway and he gave me what I found out later to be wire copy. I sat in front of a microphone, he sat in another room on the other side of a big glass window, and he listened to me as I read the wire copy for about five minutes.

Then he got up, walked in, and said, "You're hired. When can you go to work?"

Well, this changed things. Now we were negotiating. I said, "When would you like me to go to work?" He answered, "I have two men on vacation and one man sick. How about right now?" It was about 11:00 in the morning.

Now listen to this next statement. My answer must go down in the annals of the broadcasters' Hall of Fame. I've always wondered what went through his mind when I replied, with all of the aplomb of a brand new fifteen-year-old announcer, "I can't right now, Mother's waiting for me in the car."

Remember, I was just fifteen. I couldn't drive. I went down to the car, Mother drove me home, fixed me a peanut-butter and jelly sandwich, my favorite, and drove me back to the radio station. I went on the air at one o'clock that afternoon and closed the station at midnight. I knew then that I had found my "passion," that I could really be one of those "voices in the night."

The Beginning

I have been very lucky. I've been an announcer now for fifty years and I've been able to follow my passion, which led to sportscasting and thirty-seven years at the Networks. I've had the opportunity to meet, visit, and talk with stars and superstars of myriad sports around the world. I found one thing in common with all of these athletes. They may have approached it in a little different fashion, they may have had a different philosophy, they may even have come from a different culture, but the bottom line for all of them is winning. But it's more than winning. It's a way of life!

From conversations, interviews, recordings, and network experiences through the adventures of more than a half century of broadcasting, I have gathered athletes' winning thoughts and quotes to share with you in the hope that these insights will help us all become true winners. Also, along the way I've included some of my own experiences.

I hope you enjoy the journey. I have!

THE WINNERS

One of the most intriguing aspects of sports is that at the end of a contest (not unlike the end of a business day) you can look up and see exactly how you did. There's always a large scoreboard, and it tells you (and the world) whether you won or lost.

It is this clarity of athletics that is missing from so many other parts of our lives. Sometimes I feel it would be a great benefit if at the end of each telecast, a scoreboard were posted for the announcers, the directors, and the producers. Then we would all know exactly how our performance rated.

The other intriguing thing I have noticed, and it happens time and time again, is that the winners always figure out a way to win, and the losers . . . that's right, they always figure out a way to lose.

Earvin "Magic" Johnson developed the most important skill that any player, that any person can develop. He knew exactly what it was that he wanted. He knew some time in his life, very young, that he wanted to be a basketball player, and he found role models.

He modeled himself after these people and he dreamed about it all the time. He visualized himself being a great player.

That's what it's all about. It's about an image, it's about visualizing where you want to be and seeing yourself there someday. Every day you visualize it, you dream about it, you think about it, you work on it, and you keep striving for it.

The second thing that Earvin developed along the way, and it also happened to him in the very early part of his life, was that he understood what it is that all of those other people who work with him wanted out of life too. So he tried to help them become successful.

He used his skill and his ability to help James Worthy, Byron Scott, A. C. Green, all of them; he tried to help them get what they desired out of the game.

He wanted them to be All-Stars, he wanted them to make a lot of money, he wanted them to do all these things because he knew if they became successful, then the team would win and he would get everything out of life that he wanted.

I think that's the essence of Magic. He really wanted to make his teammates successful. He had no ego, he didn't care about scoring points, he didn't care about who got the publicity. The irony of the whole thing was that the more he practiced that philosophy, the more those players became successful, the more money they made individually, the more the team won, and because Earvin was the one who instigated all of these things, he got more out of it than anybody.

All of the things that you want out of life are residual benefits from winning. The real big things come from a winning team. That's why Magic is considered to be the greatest winner in the game, because he has that philosophy.

PAT RILEY is the NBA's winningest head coach, having led the L.A. Lakers to four championships, and the New York Knicks to the finals in 1994.

———

"Pat Riley and I are very similar. We want to win so badly. We want nothing else in our lives but to win."

EARVIN "MAGIC" JOHNSON
played on five championship L.A. Lakers teams.
He was the league MVP three times.

———

"There is no limit to what a man can do or where he can go if he doesn't mind who gets the credit."

ROBERT WOODRUFF,
former president of the Coca-Cola Corporation

———

John Naber

The difference in finishing first, second, or third is measured in fractions, and you can spot them, on the starting blocks.

There are three levels: there's the swimmer who is going to win and he's only concerned about what he's going to do. There's the one who is fighting to win but is probably going to finish second and he's very much concerned about what the first swimmer is going to do. And then there's the guy who is going to finish third who really doesn't care what anybody does because he's just out there on a lark.

The athletes who are going to finish first and third . . . it's easy to confuse them because they're not concerned about anybody else's business but their own.

However, the one who will win the gold medal is the one who is really expecting to perform well.

JOHN NABER won four gold medals and one silver swimming in the 1976 Olympics in Montreal. He is a 1977 Sullivan Award winner, an ABC broadcaster, and a motivational speaker.

*"If you don't know where you're going,
any road will take you there.
But once you know, then it just takes
hard work and perseverance."*

ROBERT KRAFT,
owner, New England Patriots

Frankly, the silver was my best performance in the Montreal Olympics. I didn't deserve a medal at all. I was not picked to win a medal. I was not even picked to make the final.

My silver came forty-five minutes after my first gold medal. I was the first athlete to win two individual medals on the same day and as a result, everybody sort of discounted my ability to recover in time to put in a world-class swim.

The silver medal was in the 200-meter freestyle, an event I ended up losing to American Bruce Furniss who was also a USC and USA teammate. I was like the third-place guy swimming on a lark and then ending up in second. Now, because I realize how close I was, I wonder that if I had merely put myself in a state of mind where I was "going for the gold," if I had been more focused, if I had expected wonderful things out of myself in that pool, then could I not have been just three-tenths of a second faster and thereby have won the gold medal? I don't know. I'll be haunted with that for the rest of my life. I went into that race not expecting to win, and I didn't.

*"Life is a collection
of self-fulfilling prophecies."*

JOHN NABER

14

Charlie Jones

In the late 1970s John Naber and I were cohosting the First World Cup of Swimming at Harvard University in preparation for NBC's coverage of the Moscow Olympic Games.

John on the pool deck was like the Pied Piper, particularly to the girls from the eastern bloc countries. By edict of their coaches, these swimmers were not allowed to fraternize with anyone, especially Americans, but still they followed John everywhere he went.

One of the favorites at the meet was Carmen Bunaciu of Romania, the six-foot, three-inch backstroker who would finish fourth in the 100-meter backstroke at the 1984 Los Angeles Olympics. Carmen was a gangly young lady with sharp features, and because of her height and perhaps her shyness, she had a pronounced slump.

Carmen understood English but was hesitant to speak it, as if she were afraid to be seen talking to an American. However, John had overcome all the personal and political obstacles and was setting up for a television interview with her. As he was waiting for the videotape to roll, John, who stands 6'6", turned to Carmen and said, "I've always admired tall women."

At that moment I saw a miracle take place. The ungainly duckling became the swan. Carmen stretched to her full height of 6'3", her face began to glow, and her smile reached from ear to ear. Right before our eyes she was transformed into a very attractive young lady.

Later, when I mentioned this to John Naber, he said, "I always saw Carmen as a beautiful woman."

John Wooden

I have always felt, in spite of what seems to be the general feeling, that it's easier to stay on top than it is to get there. I think it's far more difficult to get there. Once you're there, you have learned so much along the way that it puts you in a much better state of mind to stay at or near the top than it is to get there in the first place.

Perhaps it's about trying too hard. When you want something so much, I think the tendency is that you try a little too hard. You've got to learn just to make your best effort, day to day. Never think of overcoming someone else. It goes back to something my father tried to get across to me and my brothers when we were in grade school. You should never try to be better than someone else, but you should never cease to try to be the best you that you can be.

I was always trying to get my players to reach their own particular level of competency and not worry about the competency of somebody else. If theirs is higher than ours and they've worked hard, they're going to overcome. But if it's higher than ours and they haven't worked as hard as we have, then if we can come closer to our level of competency, we have a chance to overcome. I always use the positive approach. But I didn't try to sell my players a bill of goods.

JOHN WOODEN coached UCLA to ten NCAA championships in twelve years. He is the only man named to the Basketball Hall of Fame as both a coach and player.

"I try not to anticipate, just let it happen. Our whole scenario, our whole buildup with this ball club, is that we alone can destroy our championship opportunity."

PHIL JACKSON,
head coach Chicago Bulls, NBA champions

"Perseverance is how most things get done and deals get made, because eventually, most of the world will just give up."

ROBERT KRAFT

Bill Walton

Coach Wooden always taught us that it wasn't so much about competing against the opposition as it was about competing against an ideal, a level of perfection as opposed to just winning the game.

We won a lot of games, but he got most of his satisfaction—and he taught us to get most of *our* satisfaction—from playing well. Because you can play a great game and lose, and still feel good about it. You don't ever feel *great* about it, but hey, if you played well and the other team just played better, that's one thing. But if you go out there and play terribly and you get a win, you just sort of say, "Oh, God, we really stunk the place up."

The hardest time is when you're a lot better than your opponents, but you know you still have to go out there and do it. You want to come up with that great performance when there's really no challenge in terms of winning and losing. To be really great you want to come as close as you can to a brilliant performance each time, and that takes a lot of work and a lot of creative motivation.

BILL WALTON, legendary UCLA and NBA center, enjoyed a career spanning from 1974 to 1986 with Portland, San Diego, and Boston. He played on two consecutive NCAA championship teams (1972-73) and two NBA championship teams. He was College Player of the Year three times, and in 1978 was the NBA's MVP.

"You always want your opponent
to have a career day because that will elevate
your performance to a level that you didn't
know you were capable of."

GREG LOUGANIS,
arguably the greatest diver of all time, was a five-time World
Champion and was the first male diver to win two gold medals
in two consecutive Olympics: 1984 in Los Angeles, Seoul in
1988.

"I do not try to be better than anybody else.
I only try to be better than myself."

DAN JANSEN,
gold medalist and world-record setter in speed skating
at the 1994 Olympics in Lillehammer

"You never conquer the mountain, you only
conquer yourself."

JIM WHITAKER,
mountaineer, during an assault
on Mount Everest

Pat Riley

We would break our schedule down into twelve game blocks. During each one of those twelve game blocks, we'd pick out two or three real big games, games that were a little more special, like against division rivals.

But there are those other games that are strictly business. I used to call them position games. If your goal is to have the best record in the league, and you're talented enough to have the best record in the league, then there's never an excuse to lose to a team that is not as good as you are, regardless of the conditions.

I never believed in the theory that on any given night, anybody could beat you. I don't believe in that. I mean if you're better than the Spurs or the Nuggets or the Los Angeles Clippers, then you should beat them.

You drive into your players' minds that you will not tolerate mediocrity against teams that will allow you to have the best record, because you may lose against Chicago and Houston, and that's going to happen.

The way you get to be really great in this league is to defeat the teams that you're supposed to defeat, and there are never any excuses about that.

We work on that all the time and talk about it. I don't care if we're tired. I don't care if this is the third game in four nights, we're playing a team that we're better than. If we have this goal in mind, establishing our position to get the best edge in the playoffs, then we're going to win. Very rarely did we ever lose those games.

"When love and discipline come together,
you have great chemistry."

RICK PITINO,
head coach, Providence College (1985-87), New York Knicks
(1987-89), Kentucky Wildcats (1989–97) was named College
Coach of the Year three times. He is the current Head Coach of
the Boston Celtics.

"We didn't approach it as 'Let's be 13-1 in December.'
We approached it as 'Let's get this game . . .
Let's get this game . . . Let's get this game.'
The next thing you know, we were 13-1."

MICHAEL JORDAN
led the league in scoring nine times and steals three times, and
has been the NBA's MVP four times in his twelve years as a
guard for the Chicago Bulls. He has led the Bulls to five
championships and was a member of the 1984 and 1992 gold
medal–winning US Olympic teams.

Coach Wooden warned us so many times: "Don't beat yourself." When we lost at UCLA we beat ourselves.

In the pros, the other teams are so good they have more of a chance to beat you. When you're competing against someone at that level you don't really begrudge the fact that they're good players, because they put in the hours to develop their skills.

But if you're out there playing against a chump and you just can't get it done, then it eats at you for the rest of your life.

The games we lost at UCLA still eat at me, the Notre Dame game, the Oregon State game, and the North Carolina State game which cost us the championship twenty-two years ago. They will bother me until the day I die.

"You celebrate the victory,
but you analyze the defeat."

BILL WALTON

Todd Christensen

In sports, the clarity is there. You win or you lose, there are no philosophical, moral, subjective victories. There's a scoreboard.

The thing that's unique to football is that the films don't lie. You look at the films, and the players know. The films don't lie. At a certain point on the field, the films don't lie. Either you can play or you can't play.

So many times when you come from that very real world . . . I resent it when people don't talk about it as the real world, because believe me, you drag your sorry ass out there even when you have a broken bone in your foot. Don't tell me that's not the real world. That's hard. Yeah, it's well compensated, but it's hard.

What they're talking about in terms of the real world is that the clarity that exists within sports does not exist in other fields. Certainly not with the marked lucidness that it does in sport.

I'm an applause freak. I don't necessarily miss that, and I don't miss the thrill of victory and the agony of defeat, but I do miss the clarity of success, that instant validation. "Man, we won!" That's the frustration for the athlete trying to make that transition, that loss of clarity.

TODD CHRISTENSEN was an NFL All-Pro tight end for the Raiders. In a career spanning from 1979 to 1988, he set the NFL receiving record for tight ends.

Dan Fouts

It's like the scales of justice. Picture this. The left side of the scales is piled full of talent and the right side is piled full of brains. When you begin your career, it's full of the physical and almost void of the mental.

Then as you get further along in your career, it goes the other way. The balance shifts to the mental side as your physical abilities deteriorate and your mental capabilities accelerate.

The frustrating thing is, you can see your body aging right before your eyes, but you know so much more about the game and how to play it. That's really the way I always felt, especially as I got past the middle of my career. I felt, geez, I can't play forever but I'm learning more every day.

DAN FOUTS is an NFL Hall of Fame quarterback who played for the San Diego Chargers from 1973 to 1987. He threw for more than 43,000 career yards.

"The NFL is like a chess match,
where they're trying to tear your arms off."

BERNIE KOSAR
played quarterback for Cleveland, Dallas, and Miami,
from 1985 to 1996

Dan Fouts

I remember one of the first times I ever went to the sidelines for that "end of the first half two-minute warning talk" with the coaching staff. This was Don Coryell's first year [as the Chargers head coach]. He had an impressive staff as well as some impressive receivers for me to work with. On the phone was Jim Hanifan, and he's connected upstairs to Joe Gibbs and Ernie Zampese.

So I come over to the sidelines expecting to hear Coryell tell me exactly what he wants me to do. But I don't hear a word from Coryell; Hanifan's doing all the talking. Gibbs is telling him and Zampese is telling Gibbs, and the three of them are going back and forth and funneling all this information into this bewildered young quarterback.

Hanifan is telling me, "Now, on the next play, we're going to run eight-forty-four wide. You want to look at the weak safety and if the weak safety stays in the middle of the field, try to hit Charlie Joiner on the post. Now if the weak safety hangs to the weak side, then you're going to try to hit Kellan Winslow over the middle, and then there's J.J. (John Jefferson) who's running a corner. Now, if the linebackers drop back too far . . ." Hanifan's telling me all this . . . "then dump it off to Chuck Muncie underneath. Now, you got that, Dan? You got that?"

The coaches are saying, "Okay, go over it one more time. Now you got that? Joiner, Winslow, Jefferson, and then down to Muncie. Joiner, Winslow, Jefferson, Muncie."

Now, this is one of the crucial situations in the ballgame,

and I've got all this information. I start to go back out to the huddle, but I haven't heard a word from Don Coryell.

I'm thinking, "Here's the most innovative offensive coach in football, and I haven't heard a word from him. All I've done is listen to his assistants, Hanifan, Gibbs, and Zampese." Halfway out to the huddle, I feel this tug on my jersey, I turn around, and there's Coryell. I think, "Finally, he's going to tell me exactly what to do."

He said, "Screw it. Throw it to J.J."

"When it comes to crunch time,
you want to be the guy they go to."
RASHAAN SALAAM,
1994 Heisman Trophy winner and current Chicago Bear

"I always thought the easiest thing in the world
was to lead football players,
because basically they're a bunch of sheep,
and they want to please the shepherd.
They're programmed to perform
and to please whoever's in charge.
You can get them to do just about
anything you want."
DAN FOUTS

*"Leadership is not really about leading;
it's about having guys follow you.
They make the choice."*

STEVE YOUNG,
quarterback, San Francisco 49ers, 1987 to the present. He was
NFL MVP in 1992, and NFL Player of the Year in 1994.

*"I think the reason for my success
is that I was raised as a member of
a sharecropping family in the south,
and I had to take responsibility early in life."*

DON SUTTON
has chalked up 324 career victories and a 3.26 ERA in a career
spanning twenty-three years and ending in 1988. He is
currently a TV broadcaster with the Atlanta Braves.

Randy Cross

Bill Walsh gave a speech his rookie year as head coach at San Francisco, where he got up and started kind of slowly and nicely, saying, "Some of you are pretty good ballplayers, and some of you figure you can go somewhere else, and some figure, hey, if I don't make it here I can get traded."

He then stopped, and said, "I've got a news flash for you. You're on the worst team in the NFL. You were 2 and 14 last year. Who wants you? If you can't play for me and if you can't fit in with my system, you're going to be getting on with the rest of your life."

That really caught our attention.

RANDY CROSS, All-Pro offensive lineman for the 49ers (1978 to 1988), has won three Super Bowl rings. He is Charlie's former NFL broadcasting partner.

"During my rookie start as a Miami Dolphin
against the Dallas Cowboys,
I had a long conversation with myself.
Mostly I was praying,
'Dear God, don't let me get killed.'"

JIMMY CEFALO,
former Miami Dolphins wide receiver, whose career spanned
1978 to 1984, including Super Bowl XVII

Randy Cross

It all started with Bill Walsh's first practice. As an offense we knew we were on to something. It's like when you're sixteen years old and you get into a sports car for the first time. You don't know what you're doing or how you're going to drive it, but when you get behind the wheel, you say, "Oh man, this thing really goes fast." That's what our offense was like. We didn't have a defense, and we didn't know what we were doing offensively. But we were going like crazy!

The one game that turned it around for us was the New Orleans game in 1980, when we matched the previous record for the biggest comeback in the history of the league. We were down 35–7 at the half, and came back to win 38–35.

Archie Manning had just killed us in the first half, and we expected Bill to blow an aneurism on us. We went into the locker room and he just shook his head and laughed most of the time.

He said, "Look, just go out there and score a touchdown. And then stop 'em. And then score a touchdown. And then stop 'em. And if you can, score another touchdown. If you can do that, we'll get close. And if you can't do that, don't worry, you're not going to be any more embarrassed than I am already!"

Everybody sat there and said, "Well, okay. We can do that." And we did. We scored twenty-one points in the third quarter and then tied them in the fourth. It was just amazing. We went into overtime, won the toss, drove down the field, and kicked the winning field goal!

Once you establish the ability to do something like that,

it's amazing how much you can draw on it. That's the hardest challenge for any coach or manager or vice president of marketing—to be able to get that first big win, the unpredictable type of win, because then you can always draw on it.

You can always look at somebody and say, "New Orleans." They smile and laugh and say, "Yeah, that's true." We won games we had no business winning because we figured, "Hey, we did it to New Orleans; we can do it to these guys."

"We're just starting to believe we can win
football games,
and when you start believing you can win
football games,
you win them."

DENNIS ERICKSON,
head coach of the Seattle Seahawks since 1995. He was coach of the year in three different NCAA conferences, and led the University of Miami to two national championships.

"I really think it just comes down to
being mentally tough.
If things don't go well early for you,
you've got to keep going,
keep throwing the ball,
keep doing what you do best,
and things will usually come around."

DAN MARINO,
Miami Dolphins quarterback and future Hall of Famer, holds 25 NFL passing records, playing from 1983 to the present.

---

*"Confidence is only born out of one thing—
demonstrated ability. It is not born of anything
else. You cannot dream up confidence. You
cannot fabricate it. You cannot wish it. You have
to accomplish it. Macho or swaggering kinds of
confidence many times are just a coverup for
lack of confidence. I think that genuine
confidence is what you really seek for your team
and your individual players. That only comes
from demonstrated ability."*

BILL PARCELLS,
NFL head coach of the New York Giants, the
New England Patriots, and the New York Jets

"Success is never final, but failure can be."

BILL PARCELLS

Charlie Jones

In the fall of 1959 Lamar Hunt announced in *Sports Illustrated* that he was forming the American Football League. For reasons known only to myself, I decided that Lamar would need his own personal broadcaster, and I was the one to fill the bill.

I was back working at a radio station in Fort Smith, Arkansas, broadcasting all of the local high school sports that I could get my hands on. So, I gathered up my tapes, my brochure, my photos, and more biographical information than anyone would ever want and sent it all off to Lamar. I didn't hear back.

Being young and naive, I assumed my package had been lost in the mail, so I put together another box of tapes, photos, and biographical material and sent it off again. Still, I didn't hear from Lamar.

Naturally, I reasoned that the second package had also been lost in transit, so once again I put together another tape of my high school football broadcasts, photos, and biographical information, and sent it to Lamar. Still nothing.

Since the U. S. Post Office obviously was not helping my introduction to Lamar Hunt and the fledgling American Football League, I decided the only step left was a personal interview. I had a high school basketball game to broadcast in Texarkana, Arkansas, on a Friday night later in January, so I picked that as the perfect time to visit Lamar in Dallas.

My brother Ira came up with idea of sending an alarm clock to catch Lamar's attention. So we got a large, round, old-fashioned alarm clock with the two bells on top and attached a big note that said, "The Voice of the Dallas Texans will arrive in your office at eleven o'clock Saturday morning." Now keep in mind that normal business hours do not include eleven o'clock on Saturday morning, but that did not even enter our thinking.

We had to time the mailing of the package because we wanted it to arrive on Friday. We didn't want it to arrive too early, as that would kill the impact, nor did we want it to arrive the next week because then it wouldn't have any impact. Also, we didn't want it to start ticking, as then it wouldn't arrive at all. So without the service of Federal Express, UPS, or Express Mail, we tried to time the U.S. mail so the alarm clock would be there on Friday.

I drove to Texarkana, announced the basketball game Friday night, and after a few hours' sleep left at four o'clock in the morning for Dallas. I didn't want to be late for my eleven o'clock appointment. I wasn't. I arrived in downtown Dallas at eight A.M. Naturally I had some time to kill, so I parked across the street from Neiman-Marcus and proceeded to do some window shopping.

In addition to sending the alarm clock, my brother and I also decided that since I was going to be in Texas I should be wearing a ten-gallon Stetson hat. I was. As I walked around downtown Dallas early that Saturday morning, it became very apparent that I was the only person in downtown Dallas wearing a cowboy hat.

Finally, eleven o'clock arrived, and I stepped into the Dallas Texans' office on the first floor of the Mercantile Bank Building. I was greeted by Lamar's receptionist, who took one look at the cowboy hat and said, "You have to be Charlie Jones. Lamar got your clock, and he's eager to meet

you." Now you can imagine all of the great thoughts that
were just waiting to be thought when she added, "However,
there's a meeting of the eight owners of the American
Football League teams, and Lamar won't be able to see you
until four o'clock tomorrow afternoon."

My face must have shown the extent of my pocketbook,
which at that time contained a total of $6, just enough to
buy gas to get me back to Fort Smith. She immediately
brightened my spirits with the words, "We have a
reservation for you at the Hilton Hotel, and we'll pay for
your room. Sign for dinner and breakfast, and Lamar will
see you tomorrow afternoon."

I stayed over, and we had a delightful meeting on
Sunday, outlining all the parameters of my becoming the
"Voice of the Dallas Texans," with additional duties of
promoting the team and the American Football League.
Lamar said he would contact me the next day, and I drove
back to Fort Smith on a great high.

Lamar called me at noon Monday and said the job was
mine; how soon could I come to work? I said, "Two weeks.
I need to give the owner of the radio station two weeks
notice. I'll let you know the exact date tomorrow."

The next day I had lunch with the station owner, who
informed me that since I was going to leave anyway, then I
could just make this my last day. After lunch I was cleaning
out my desk when Lamar called.

"How did it go?" he asked. I didn't know how to reply,
so there was this long pause. Lamar laughed, "You got
fired, didn't you?" Another long pause. "Don't worry. I'll
put you on the payroll today and you get down here next
Monday."

*"There are no limitations if you broaden
your horizons.
If you don't succeed you haven't failed,
because you cannot fail if you've tried
your hardest."*

CARL LEWIS,
is one of America's greatest Olympic track and field stars,
winner of nine gold medals and one silver medal at four
consecutive Olympic games.

*"If what you want
does not happen for you right away,
stay at it.
Become good at it.
You'll be surprised
at how your confidence will build
as you develop self-discipline."*

TERRY BRADSHAW,
Hall of Famer, quarterbacked the Pittsburgh Steelers to four
Super Bowl championships. His career spanned from
1970 to 1983. He is now an NFL sportscaster
with the Fox network.

Pat Riley

Teamwork in business is the ultimate contradiction. When management says we have to have so many dollars every year in sales in order for us to be successful, then when that is achieved as a group, even though the individuals are doing it, they have to give something back to the group.

I think that's where there's a problem. Management is always worried about the bottom line. They keep trying to motivate and inspire the troops to achieve a goal so they can have great sales, but do they really give back to those individuals? Unless they give some of it back, in bonuses or profits, then those people will take a very cynical approach.

Teamwork, to me, is the essence of life. It is in sports as it is in business as it is in a family. I think individuals that work for a company won't buy into teamwork unless they're going to get something back themselves. It's just human nature.

Now, if you're going to pay somebody $8 an hour and they're going to bust their ass and you're going to achieve your goal as a company but you just give them a "thank you," then after awhile they won't be as productive. Everybody has to share in that. They really do.

That's what leadership is about. Leadership is defining reality and telling the truth. If the leaders aren't going to tell these people the truth, if they're going to keep large smoke screens around them then eventually they're going to get the message and say, "Hey, they don't care about us.

They just want us to work hard so they can achieve the bottom line and make the stockholders happy, but we get nothing out of this." Then eventually the morale will drop, and there won't be any spirit.

---

*"The team concept cannot be duplicated
in business.
In professional sports, once you make the
starting line-up there's no chance for advancement;
you're already there.
So the only chance for advancement
is for the team to win -
then everybody wins."*

BOB TRUMPY
was an All-Pro NFL tight end with the Cincinnati Bengals
from 1968 to 1977 and currently works as an NFL analyst
on NBC Sports.

---

*"Truly great actors go out of their way
to make sure the supporting actors are brilliant,
because they want the play to be great.
These are the people who really understand
the essence of leadership and teamwork."*

PAT RILEY

*"We're better off when we realize it takes all five
guys to make the wagon roll."*

CHARLES OAKLEY,
gutsy forward, New York Knicks

*"Winning is not as important as playing
as well as you can."*

BEN TURK,
six-foot, ten-inch cello-playing center for the NCAA
Division III Cal Tech Beavers basketball team—the
smartest team in America

"Victory is not necessarily a gold medal."

GALE TANGER,
U.S. figure skating judge

John Wooden

I didn't want my players to have to log a lot of hours watching films or worrying about other things. That's my job: to get everything organized in such a way that during practice we get it all done.

My feeling was, and it has never changed, that intercollegiate athletics, interscholastic athletics, are just a small part of their lives. The important part is their education.

Basketball is to be from the time we start practice until we end it, and I wanted them to know that they'd better be there on time, but they had every right to know that we're also going to quit on time. We're not going to go a minute over, and we're not going to start a minute late.

"TV has made actors
out of players, coaches, and officials.
There's far more showmanship.
If I wanted showmanship,
I'd go see the Globetrotters."

JOHN WOODEN

Charlie Jones

I remember vividly the first time I met Lew Alcindor (Kareem Abdul-Jabbar). It was at the NCAA Western Regional Finals, during one of UCLA's championship runs.

I was trying to figure out a way to relate his size to our viewers at home without it getting lost in the translation of television. I thought I had the perfect analogy when I came up with a common denominator that most viewers could relate to, his shirt size. I went up to Lew after practice on Friday and asked: "What size dress shirt do you wear?" His answer was what I later found to be typical of most superstars, even in college: "Man, I don't know. They're all custom made."

"I just want my son to be himself
and realize the potential he finds within himself."

KAREEM ABDUL-JABBAR
is the NBA's all-time leader in points scored, games played, and
years played. His career spanned 1969 to 1988 with Milwaukee
and Los Angeles. He has won six MVP awards, three NBA
championships, and three NCAA championships at UCLA.

Bill Walton

So much of basketball is anticipation, what you think is going to happen. That's why Larry Bird, in my opinion, is the quickest basketball player.

When you think about players who are quick, you don't think about Larry Bird, but in my mind Larry's the quickest player because he knows what's going to happen before it happens. It's his sense of anticipation, his sense of analysis, his work done before the game, so that when it happens, he's already been through it in his mind and then it's just execution.

When I played with Larry Bird, I'd always tell myself, "Just keep going, just keep going." Plus, when you're playing with great players, like we had on the Celtics, you only had to do your part because everybody else was doing their part and if you try to do too much, you'll run into them, and you didn't want to do that.

With all those great players, we could actually extend our control of the game beyond the court. The action is only on the court but we could extend the force of our game into the crowd to where we could get them to want us to win, even though they were rooting for the other team. We would play so well that they would become fans of ours.

That's tough to believe. Some teams have fans because they win. Other teams have hometown fans. Still other teams have fans because of the style they play.

When you go into their arena, your opponents want more than anything else to beat you. Their whole life is to beat you at that one game. If by the end of the game you've

41

just humiliated them, because you've destroyed them, their fans will stay and they will appreciate your performance. They'll actually cheer for you. They cheer the great players.

"To play at the top of your game is the easy part.
Anytime you want to, you can go out
and pad your numbers,
but to win you have to have
everybody around you playing great."

BILL WALTON

"I don't think there's anything
that replaces a competitive sport.
If I play anything, my mind gets on what I'm
doing and I really work at it.
But I don't find that in business.
Business, to me, is more common sense."

JACK NICKLAUS
is the all-time leader in major championships (twenty), has won the Masters six times (more than any other golfer), and the PGA Championship five times.

Pat Riley

First of all, you teach players that losing is just as much a part of the game as winning. I used to set a reverse goal. We'd come into training camp and I would say to my players, "It's okay to lose twenty-five games."

Now twenty-five games to most people seems like a lot of losing. But you must realize that twenty-five losses adds up to fifty-seven victories, which means you'd probably win your division and your conference and have the best record in the league.

So they have to understand that losing is just as much a part of the game as winning.

*"I don't want to be on the team
that wins seventy games and doesn't win
the championship.
I'd rather be on a team that wins fifty and wins
the championship."*

MICHAEL JORDAN

*"To win, you have to lose,
and then get pissed off."*

JOE NAMATH
was a quarterback with the N.Y. Jets and the L.A. Rams from 1965 to 1977. He was named Super Bowl III MVP in 1969 after he "guaranteed" the Jets' victory.

43

*"In baseball you can't let losing carry over
to the next day.
You've got to flip the page."*

DON BAYLOR,
an All-Star and MVP as a player, is the current manager of the
Colorado Rockies.

*"I cannot get rid of the hurt from losing . . .
but after the last out of every loss,
I must accept that there'll be a tomorrow.
In fact, it's more than there'll be a tomorrow;
it's that I want there to be a tomorrow.
That's the big difference. I want tomorrow
to come."*

SPARKY ANDERSON,
now retired, was one of baseball's winningest managers,
skipper of the Cincinnati Reds and
the Detroit Tigers for twenty-five years.

*"Life to me is about challenges and climbing
mountains. I don't like to live in the past.
The past is for cowards."*

MIKE DITKA,
Super Bowl–winning head coach of the Chicago Bears, is
now head coach of the New Orleans Saints.

Johnny Bench

I call it inner conceit, knowing that I was better than the other player in a situation. If I went to the plate, he wasn't going to get me out. I was going to win the ballgame, or I was going to hit the ball out of the ballpark.

I think the one thing you need, especially when you're in a team sport, is complete confidence that they can hit it to the shortstop, they can hit it to the center fielder, that the pitcher doesn't have to strike out this guy, that if he just gets the ball put in play then somebody will make the play. It was a total confidence among eight special individuals every time we went out there.

And if we hold them within a certain number, if we were within two runs in the sixth or seventh inning, we had them, because our bullpen was going to hold them and we were going to score runs. They just didn't make pitchers who could hold us.

Everybody thinks baseball's a team game, but it's all individual as far as I'm concerned. If you have eight great individuals that have set goals and they are good enough to reach those goals, that individually if you play your position, if you perform at the plate, then you're going to turn out a team win. But remember, in baseball it's individual performances that create a team win.

JOHNNY BENCH, Hall of Famer, was one of the greatest catchers in baseball history. In his seventeen years with the Reds, he was named Rookie of the Year, league MVP twice, and World Series MVP in 1976.

*"My responsibility is to get my twenty-five guys
playing for the name on the front of their uniform
and not the one on the back."*

TOMMY LASORDA,
now retired, spent his entire career with the Brooklyn/Los
Angeles Dodgers as a player, coach, and manager.

*"Greg Maddux does more than throw baseballs.
What Larry Bird did, what Joe Montana did,
Greg Maddux now does.
He sees possibilities no one else sees and
he makes them real in ways that create beauty."*

DAVE KINDRED
is a sports columnist with the *Atlanta Journal Constitution.*

"Greg Maddux is a thinking man's pitcher,
only he doesn't think as a pitcher.
He thinks as a hitter."

CHARLIE O'BRIEN

has had the privilege of catching the Braves' Maddux, as well as pitchers for the A's, the Brewers, the Mets, and the Blue Jays.

"People judge too much by results.
I'm just the opposite.
I care about more than results.
I'd rather make a good pitch and
give up a bloop single
than make a bad pitch and get an out."

GREG MADDUX

won the Cy Young award for four consecutive years with two teams, the Cubs and the Braves.

Dave Winfield

At the Major League level, everybody has ability, but some people don't have the mental toughness, don't have it day to day, don't really have the desire. You can enhance what you already have. But if you don't have it in the first place, it's tough to get it.

There are a lot of complacent people in baseball. A lot of easygoing people. A lot of people who are not hungry because they come from a middle-class, easygoing background, and they've got a job and they execute and they don't really have high goals or aspirations because they have a comfortable level of success. There are a lot of those people in the game.

I wasn't born with a silver spoon in my mouth. I learned I had a combative instinct in me. I don't like being embarrassed, I don't like being hurt, so if a guy does something to me I'm coming back on him. A lot of times I'm getting him first. Most of the time I'm getting him first, but there aren't a lot of players who could tell you they feel the same way. There's a difference.

Sometimes it's guys from the Dominican Republic who know they don't have many alternatives. It's this, the sugar cane fields, or die.

You have a lot of players in the United States who've had it easy and they have a different kind of competitiveness. They know the techniques and the fundamentals, but the drive to succeed and be on top isn't there. I've seen it. I've seen it a lot.

"I have trouble as an employer.
If my employees don't put out
like I know I put out,
and they're not giving it everything,
then I think they're cheating me."

DAVE WINFIELD,
future baseball Hall of Famer, enjoyed a career spanning
twenty-three seasons. In 1992 he became the only
forty-year-old to drive in more than one hundred
RBIs in a season.

"The media generation has infiltrated
the souls of the young
with too much instant gratification.
Only when life is difficult is there
a hunger to succeed.
We've gotten away from that;
I wonder when it will all stop."

MELVIN STEWART,
1992 Olympic gold medalist and former world-record
holder in the 200-meter butterfly, a fourteen-time
U.S. national champion

Most people are generally selfish, and they're afraid. It's called the disease of "me."

Most people go into everything looking out for their own ass. They're looking out for themselves, and they'll say all the right things and give you a lot of lip service, but they're taking care of number one.

There's nothing wrong with that but you'll never be part of something truly significant if that's going to be your attitude. You have to change.

*"In basketball,
you can be the greatest player in the world
and lose every game,
because a team will always beat an individual."*

BILL WALTON

*"Losing does nothing but make you feel bad
and inadequate."*

PAT RILEY

Tony Gwynn

There were always coaches who said that I couldn't do something. I couldn't throw, I couldn't hit with power, I couldn't run, I couldn't field my position.

I think that's one of the reasons I've been successful, because they can measure everything you do on the field, but they cannot measure what's inside of you and what drives you.

It's easy to cheat yourself and do just enough to get by, but that's what everybody can do, just enough to get by. But those who want to be successful and maintain that level of success have got to push a little bit harder and do a little bit more.

TONY GWYNN, seven-time National League batting champion, has been playing for the San Diego Padres since 1982.

"I don't worry about not hitting.
I go to the plate every night
and I take my bat with me."

TERRY PENDLETON,
who since 1984 has played third base for the Cardinals, Braves,
and Marlins, was National League MVP in 1991.

"There'll be two buses leaving the hotel
for the ballpark tomorrow.
The 2 p.m. bus will be for those of you
who need a little extra work.
The empty bus will leave at 5 p.m."

DAVE BRISTOL,
from 1966 to 1980, managed the Reds, Brewers, Braves,
and Giants.

"Let's be honest.
We're losing by eight runs,
and all I'm thinking about at that point
is getting back to the hotel by midnight
because that's when room service closes.
All of a sudden we start getting hits and more
hits, and I'm saying, 'I'm not going to make it.'
If you're not going to get back in time for room
service, then you might as well win."

JOHN KRUK
played for the Padres, White Sox and Phillies. He retired
in 1995 after being diagnosed with testicular cancer.

Charlie Jones

I first started announcing baseball in 1965 when I joined Bill Mercer for the radio broadcasts of the Dallas-Fort Worth Spurs in the Texas League.

This was during the time when minor league announcers didn't travel with the team. We did re-creations from the radio studio when the ball club was on the road. To spice up our broadcasts, we had a great audio engineer who filled in the crowd noise, the sounds of the vendors, the sound of the ball hitting the bat, plus several of his own creations.

When the Spurs were in El Paso, in the Mountain time zone, at eight o'clock at night our engineer would ring the Mission Bells near the ballpark. However, he would only ring seven bells because of the time change between El Paso and Dallas. Also, the ballpark was near the airport, so he was always playing recordings of planes landing and taking off. (One night he got carried away, and we had a World War II dogfight over the El Paso Airport.)

Our budget was so small we couldn't afford the wire service, so we hired a high school kid in each city for $10 a game. He called us at the end of the first inning, then after the third, the sixth, and the ninth. He had permission to add one more phone call if there was a real long inning, or extra innings, so that we didn't get too far behind. We'd always start our broadcast about fifteen minutes behind the actual baseball game so we had some leeway.

The information he would give us read like this:

Young, 2-2, flies out to right
Kessinger, 1st pitch, out, 6-3
Johnson, struck out, three straight pitches.

This was what we had to work with and the rest was up to us. We would create the full inning, take each pitch and play around with it. We would weave in our statistics, anecdotes and stories. The beauty of this was that we controlled the tempo of the game. If we had a really great story we wanted to share, we could tell it at length because we could foul off as many pitches as we wanted to, until we had completed the punch line. We never let the truth interfere with a good story.

Now, all was going along rather smoothly until the second month of the season. The Spurs were playing the Braves, in Austin, Texas, and in the sixth inning the phone lines went down in the Austin press box. We had nowhere to go.

So, Bill and I quickly became very creative. We announced to our listeners that a snake had started to work its way through the holes in the screen behind home plate. As it slithered and weaved its way in and out of the screen, the fans directly behind home plate naturally started screaming and hollering and moving away from the snake (our engineer had appropriate screams, hollers, and chair scraping noise). This caught the attention of the players and also the attention of the home plate umpire, who called time (our engineer used his own voice: 'Time! Time out! What's going on back there?') and came over to see what was happening.

The players came out of both dugouts, and formed this semicircle at home plate, all looking at the screen and watching the snake. It looked like it was a water moccasin, and of course, if it was a water moccasin, then it could be very dangerous. (Background of people milling around and mumbling.)

The groundskeeper didn't want to have anything to do with the snake, so he called the Austin Humane Society (phone dialing), and this took some time before the Humane Society could get there (appropriate sirens). Finally, two men arrived (slamming of car doors) and climbed up two long ladders (footsteps on wooden ladders) with two long poles with pinchers on the end (snap, snap). Every time they would try to snare the snake behind its head, it would slither away and weave itself through another hole in the screen. (Oh's and ah's from players and fans.)

We spent about twenty minutes making up the snake story before the phone lines were finally fixed in Austin. As soon as the phone lines were up and running, and we knew what was really going on in the game, the two men from the Humane Society caught the snake (applause), put it in a box (slam shut), and they were out of there (Humane Society truck's engine backfired as it pulled away from the ball park) and Bill and I went back to the real broadcast.

"Life is full of hills. . . . Some days it's uphill . . . some days it's downhill . . . mostly it's side hill."

CHARLIE BROWN,
in a "Peanuts" cartoon

---

*"The U.S. golfers are like thoroughbred sheep.
They are tremendously bred and trained, and
they run correctly, but the problem is that they
are still sheep, and sheep want to be part of the
flock. We need guys who are willing to say, 'The
flock is fine and it is a nice place to be and it is
comfortable, and we are all very rich and
enjoying the bounties of the flock. But the hell
with the flock; I want to be a wolf.' "*

JOHNNY MILLER
has won twenty-three PGA Tour championships, and was the
1973 U.S. Open champion.

*"What I have learned about myself is that
I am an animal when it comes to achievement
and wanting success. There is never
enough success for me."*

GARY PLAYER,
international star, winner of all four major
golf championships

Johnny Miller

I think the difference between first and second place is clear intention. Intention is the magical word. When you go to a golf tournament, you need to ask yourself, "What is my intention? Why am I here? Am I here to have a good time, am I here to play a level of golf never seen before, am I here to make the cut, am I here to make some money to pay the bills?" You need to tune that intention to a level that is just slightly out of your reach.

We had a famous man in our church who said, "Always lengthen your stride." In other words, if you just stride so that it's comfortable, you'll never improve. You always have to stretch the muscles just slightly. You can't stretch them too much or you'll get injured.

That's the secret of really being great. If you lengthen your stride and you even hurt a little bit once in awhile because you're striving for one more level of excellence, your eyes will be opened and you'll gain more intelligence and you'll gain more understanding.

The players who do that, who become great, are the ones who are willing to take a gamble on a shot where everybody thinks, "You shouldn't take that gamble. It's safer to go over here." Then everybody plays safe or they choke into the water. But the player who wins tournaments is the one who's willing to say, "My intention here is not to play smart, not to play safe, but to win."

My intention is to do what others are not willing to do, and sometimes that equates to a tough shot over water to a tight pin. You can do it. It's in your repertoire, and if you can pull off those shots, that's what makes you win tournaments, not accidentally win them.

A lot of people accidentally win tournaments on the tour. The great champion wins tournaments. He clearly goes out and wins the tournament. People don't say, "Well, he was lucky. He got a good break. He double bogied the last hole, and backed in." You just go out and you win because you have the formula.

"We all choke.
You're not human if you haven't.
We get just as nervous as the average guy
playing for the club championship."

CURTIS STRANGE,
a four-time member of the U.S. Ryder Cup team, has chalked up seventeen tour victories since 1976. He was back-to-back U.S. Open champion in 1988 and 1989.

---

*"God gave me this gift
and He can take it away just as quick.
I don't want to tempt Him by not practicing.
There's nothing else I'd rather do than play golf."*

LEE TREVINO
has had much success as a PGA and Senior PGA golfer,
winning two U.S. Opens, two British Opens, and two PGA
Championships.

*"There's no such thing as a natural touch.
Touch is something you create
by hitting millions of golf balls."*

LEE TREVINO

*"My goal was not to work harder than anybody
else. My goal was to beat everybody else.
It still is."*

TOM KITE
1989 PGA Player of the Year and 1992 U.S. Open champion.

Lee Trevino

How about we go back a little bit. I learned to play golf at Tennyson Park Golf Links in Dallas, Texas. I worked extremely hard at my game, and I got very good at it. I used to hustle at Tennyson Park with all the boys. I got to the point where I couldn't find a game, because I would go around in 65 - 64 - 66 each and every day.

Then in 1965 I got a call to go out to El Paso to play a match with Fred Hawkins, and I got introduced to Martin Lettage and all the "cotton farmers" as I called them. I beat Fred in two rounds, and they said, "Why don't you move out here? You've out-hustled everybody in Dallas, come on out here. Nobody really knows you." So I did.

A few months later I was working in the pro shop at Horizon Hills Country Club, and one of the guys walked in. He said, "How you doing?" I said "Fine." I hadn't seen him in a year. He said, "I hear all these 'cotton farmers' out here have a lot of money and like to bet on you."

I said, "Well, generally they'll back me against anybody I'll play." He said, "Do you think they would bet if you played a touring pro?" And I said, "I don't see why not." He said, "How about Raymond Floyd?" Now Raymond Floyd was twenty-two years old; he'd already won at St. Petersburg, his first PGA tournament victory.

So they brought Raymond Floyd out. I didn't know Raymond Floyd; Raymond Floyd didn't know Lee Trevino. Raymond Floyd drove up in a brand new, white, shiny Cadillac. We didn't even have pavement on our parking lot. It was kind of crushed white rock.

I saw the car drive up, so I took a cart, and drove out to meet him. I took Raymond Floyd's big Wilson bag out of the trunk, with all the shoes in it and all the extra clubs, and then took it into the locker room. I took his shoes, shined his shoes, and brought the shoes back to him. He looked up at me and said, "By the way, who am I playing today?" I said, "Me."

Raymond looked at me, and said, "You gotta be joking." One of the fellows walked into the locker room and said to Raymond, "Hey, you want to go look at the golf course before you play this guy?" We're playing at noon. Raymond said, "No. I'm playing the shoeshine boy. I'm a professional golfer. I don't need to go out there and look at the golf course." So he went in and had breakfast and played a little gin, and I went out to the practice tee.

We played. Well, to make a long story short, I shot 65, and I beat Raymond pretty bad that day. He wanted to play an emergency nine, but I said, "Mr. Floyd, I can't play another nine holes, because I have to put the carts up." He said, "That's about right. I'm playing the cart man." You see, I did everything around the club.

The next day we came out, and I beat Raymond again. Then the third day, which was the final day, Raymond doubled up and pressed and everything and we tied the front nine and Raymond eagled the last hole to beat me one up. And I'll never forget what Raymond said when he pulled the ball out of the hole. He looked at the ball and he looked at his backers, and he said, "Boys, I can find an easier game on the tour."

I remember when Raymond went back out on tour, he said, "I just played a little Mexican boy down in El Paso, Texas, that you all are going to have to make some room for when he gets out here." Raymond and I have been great friends ever since.

*"It's amazing how many people beat you at golf
once you're no longer president."*

GEORGE BUSH,
former President of the United States

*"I learn more from victory, because
I have trained myself to concentrate on the good
and the positive."*

HALE IRWIN
won nineteen PGA Tour events, including three
U.S. Opens, and is among the leading money
winners on the Senior PGA tour.

"I am a winner. I just didn't win today."

GREG NORMAN,
"the Shark," is golf's reigning superstar and one of the
sport's most charismatic players. He led the PGA in
winnings on 1986 and 1990, and is the
winner of two British Opens.

Charlie Jones

Lee Trevino and I anchored NBC's golf for several years, and we really had a great time together. Most of all I remember a conversation that took place during a Friday rehearsal on the tower at the eighteenth green at Onion Creek Country Club in Austin, Texas, the site of the Legends of Golf.

That afternoon I had called my brother Ira, in Fort Smith, Arkansas, to see how he was getting along. In our conversation, he told me of the struggles they were having with the Girls' Shelter. He was a former president of the association and was on the board of directors of the shelter, which is a halfway house for abused teenage girls. Due to the fact that both the state and the federal governments had been cutting back on their funding, it was becoming a struggle for the shelter to survive.

After I hung up, Lee asked me about the conversation and I explained it to him. Lee immediately said, "Let's do something for them." I said, "What do you have in mind?" Lee said, "Why don't I put on an exhibition." I said, "Lee, that would be fantastic, but you get $35,000 for an exhibition. There's just no way that we could raise that kind of money in a town the size of Fort Smith." "Oh, no," he said, "I'll donate my time. I'll do it for free. We'll get the home pro, a local amateur, and the best young high school player in a foursome, we'll play an exhibition, and we'll raise some money for the Girls' Shelter."

We went to Fort Smith, played the exhibition, and it was a huge success. Lee had a great time, and after it was over, he said, "I'll come back next year, we'll do it again, but let's make it a little bigger."

So the next year we added an amateur tournament, and we raised even more money, and Lee said, "I'll come back next year." He wanted to help the local club pros in western Arkansas and eastern Oklahoma, so we added a $10,000 pro tournament, a clinic, and an auction. We raised more money. Lee continued coming back for five years.

Over that period of time Lee Trevino raised more than $250,000 for the Girls' Shelter, which means there will always be money to help abused teenage girls in Fort Smith, Arkansas.

I once asked Lee, "Why are you doing this?" He said, "Golf has been so good to me; this is the way I give back to the game. Seven or eight times a year, I'm involved in projects just like this in different parts of the country. There's not a lot of publicity involved. I don't want any publicity. It's my way of giving back to the game of golf."

"The only thing wrong with the Senior Tour
is there is too much sitting around time.
I wish we played two tournaments every week,
one on Monday, Tuesday, and Wednesday,
and the other on Friday, Saturday, and Sunday."

LEE TREVINO

"A golfer can't dictate what his opponents shoot.
He can't wave his arms or tackle a playing
partner who's getting ready to putt.
But he can always reach within himself
to bring out the best in his battle
against the laws of physics and par."

ARNOLD PALMER
won the Masters four times and the British Open twice, as well
as the U.S. Open. He was named PGA Player of the Year twice,
and was the first golfer to surpass $1 million in career earnings.

"When a golfer changes his putter,
things might go well for about a week
because having something new
gives him confidence.
But then the new putter gets to know him,
and things turn sour again.
It's the Indian, not the arrow."

LEE TREVINO

Charlie Jones

The year was 1969, and I was at the Firestone Country Club in Akron, Ohio, stationed at the seventeenth green of the old World Series of Golf. This was a thirty-six-hole affair over Labor Day weekend, featuring the winners of the four major golf championships, and from there I was scheduled to go to New York City for NBC's football meetings.

Several of us were having breakfast on Sunday including Arnold Palmer, who was NBC's guest analyst. Arnie suggested that rather than flying home to California and then flying back to New York that I join him and Winnie in Latrobe, Pennsylvania, as a house guest for a couple of days. So after the event was over Sunday afternoon we boarded his Lear jet and flew to Latrobe.

The following night I met his neighbors Tom and Mary Moran, who joined us for dinner and afterwards a bridge game. I must tell you, that even though I love to play, I'm a terrible bridge player. I played horribly and barely managed to get through the evening. I was really embarrassed by my performance. I choked.

Well, this weighed heavily on my mind because I knew that the next spring I would be going back to Latrobe, where NBC was covering the tournament at Ligonier, Pennsylvania, which is just down the road. I knew that in all likelihood I would be involved in another bridge game with Arnold Palmer, Mary Moran, and Tom Moran.

Therefore, in the few months that I had before going back, I created a crash course in bridge preparation. I read half a dozen bridge books. I made up hands and read every newspaper bridge lesson I could find and honed what little bit of talent I had to a fine edge.

Now we fast forward. It's next May, I go in for the telecast, and lo and behold, on Wednesday night before the tournament's to start, the fatal bridge game gets underway.

Now I must also say with all candor that at this point I was playing very well, and that all of my diligence was paying off. Tom and I were partners. Arnie was partnered with Mary. We started at about seven-thirty that evening with the stipulation that we'd only play until eleven because Arnie had an eight-o'five tee time the next morning. We had a very nice evening of bridge, and when the clock struck eleven, Arnie was losing, so we played on.

It became midnight, Arnie was still losing, so we played on. One o'clock in the morning, Arnie was still losing, so we played on. Two o'clock in the morning, Arnie was still losing, and at this time he got up to go to the bathroom.

As soon as Arnie left the room my partner Tom Moran leaned across the bridge table and said, "Charlie, we've got to start losing." I said, "What do you mean, we've got to start losing?" And Tom said, "If we don't lose and Arnie doesn't get ahead, we're going to be here all night long, and remember, Arnie's got a golf tournament to play, and he has an eight-o'five tee time in the morning."

Arnie came back, we played a few more hands, we lost, Arnie took the lead, and as soon as he did, he put his cards face-down on the table and said, "Well, that wraps it up for me. I've got to get some rest. Remember, I've got an eight-o'five tee time in the morning."

And that was the end of my killer bridge game with Arnold Palmer.

*"I'd rather win one tournament in my life
than make the cut every week."*

ARNOLD PALMER

*"The real competitor is not easy to live with,
when he is on his way up, and when he is at the top,
because he is driven to compete with everyone,
he wants to do everything better,
he wants to dominate everyone around him —
his friends, his associates, his employers, his wife.
This is the deepest need in his nature
and allowance must be made for it.
It has made him what he is;
without it, we would never have heard of him."*

STIRLING MOSS
is a ten-time Great Britian Grand Prix champion race driver. In
a career spanning fourteen years, he won 194 of the 466 races
he entered.

*"Every time I play, in my own mind I'm the
favorite."*

TIGER WOODS,
three-time U.S. Amateur champion, 1996 PGA Tour
Rookie of the Year, and 1997 Masters champion

*"I've played a couple of hundred games
of tick-tack-toe with my little daughter,
and she hasn't beaten me yet.
I've always had to win. I've got to win."*

BOB GIBSON,
one of the greatest right-handed pitchers of all time, was the
World Series and Cy Young award winner twice. In 1968 he
won both the Cy Young and the MVP awards by logging the
lowest national ERA (1.12) and thirteen shutouts.

"I'm about winning."

EARVIN "MAGIC" JOHNSON
played on five championship L.A. Lakers teams. He was also an
All-Star eight consecutive seasons, and the league MVP three
times. He was an Olympic gold medalist in 1992.

*"I think mental toughness is the difference
in this League in being successful.
I just think you let the competition take over.
If you gear yourself to the competition,
whether it's the one-on-one, hitter-pitcher,
or team against team,
that's where you'll get measured."*

TONY LARUSSA,
the fifth lawyer to manage in the Major Leagues, has had
much success since 1983, as skipper of the White Sox,
the Oakland A's, and the St. Louis Cardinals.

Charlie Jones

In 1966, the second year that I was with NBC Sports, I drew one of the premier assignments, the Bob Hope Chrysler Classic in the Palm Springs area. The reason this was so choice is at that time Chrysler Corporation was the sole sponsor of the Bob Hope Classic, and also the sponsor of half of all sports on NBC. So it was, and still is, a heavyweight event for the network.

I was living in Dallas, and when I got the news I called my friend, the great golfer Mickey Wright, to have lunch and to discuss the Bob Hope Classic. Mickey filled me in on the players, the background of the tournament, and the four golf courses it would be played on. I then read everything I could find, the complete PGA tour guide, and all the golf magazines so that when I got to Palm Springs I would be ready. I had information coming out of my suitcases.

Saturday we were broadcasting from La Quinta. We were on for one hour, and I was stationed at the bottom of the tower at 18. I was to read the opening billboards ("The Bob Hope Classic is brought to you by Chrysler," etc., etc., etc.). Then I was to do an update at the thirty-minute mark, some interviews near the end of the hour telecast, and then take us off the air.

At the top of the show, I read the opening billboards, which lasted twenty seconds, and that was the last thing I did. I waited and waited and waited, but they never came back to me. I was absolutely devastated. I went back to my room at the Erawan Garden Hotel, which is still going strong on Highway 111, and went into hiding. I was so embarrassed that I didn't even feel like venturing out of my room.

Suddenly, the phone rang, and it was Mickey Wright. She said, "Charlie, you were absolutely fantastic." I said, "Mickey, how can you say that? I only did twenty seconds." She said, "But you did them so well." Then she added, "I learned a long time ago only to worry about the things I can control. When I'm playing in a golf tournament, I can only worry about my golf game and not what the other golfers might be doing. So you need only concern yourself with what you did when they came to you, and that was for twenty seconds, and you were magnificent." Well, of course, this really buoyed my spirits, so I went back to work, gathering even more background material for the next day.

On Sunday, I was at the fifteenth hole at Indian Wells, and I had enough notes taped to the scaffolding, the monitor, and the table that I could have talked for three hours on that hole alone. I remember even today, thirty years later, it's the famous par three with an hour-glass shaped green. They called it the $50,000 hole, where Don January had the first hole-in-one insured by Lloyds of London; it was "The Golf Shot Heard Around the World."

As we came on the air, I was again to read the opening billboards. As I announced "The Bob Hope Desert Classic is brought to you by Chrysler," etc., etc., etc., the last threesome of the day was putting out on 15. When I got through the opening billboards, that was it. There were no more golfers. They were all on 16, 17, and 18. I was crushed again. How could this possibly happen two days in a row?

Then, the best turn of events that a golf announcer at the fifteenth hole can ever have, Arnold Palmer and Doug Sanders tied, and they headed for sudden death.

The first playoff hole is the par-3 fifteenth.

My hole.

I'm ready.

While Arnie and Doug were being driven out, our director punched up a shot of Dwight Eisenhower who was in the gallery at 18. This was the first year the Eisenhower Trophy was to be awarded, and the general was there to make the presentation. Our producer, Lou Kusserow, shouted in my ear, "Monitor, monitor." So naturally I looked at the monitor and he then said, "There's the LATE president." Well, I knew that the word "late" was incorrect, but I could not think of the word "former." And in the process of trying to remember "former," I forgot the man's name. However, I quickly recovered with the statement, "THERE HE IS." There was this long silence in my ear, followed by several expletives from Lou.

The players were now on the tee at 15, and I waxed eloquent about the hole. Doug Sanders hit his tee shot on the green and Arnie missed the green and was down the right side, below the trap.

As the golfers walked up the fairway, Lou Kusserow decided he would try it again and shouted in my ear, "Monitor, monitor." I looked at the monitor, and he said in a very strident voice, "The LATE president." Again I knew that "late" was incorrect, I still could not think of the word "former," and in the process, I still could not remember the name of perhaps, at that time, the most famous man in the world, so I said, "THERE HE IS, AGAIN."

Author's note: Doug Sanders parred the hole, Arnie bogied, Sanders won, and Lou Kusserow never again called for a shot of the former president, Dwight David Eisenhower when I was announcing.

"General Eisenhower was certainly a better player than the average American who played golf. He hit the ball pretty well, but the strongest part of his game was his desire. Richard Nixon wasn't really a golfer. Gerald Ford had an eighteen handicap and deserved every bit of it, but he hit the ball hard. Ford's problem was, he had the yips putting. George Bush plays to a fourteen handicap, and now that he has more free time, I think his game will get better. Bill Clinton has the potential to be a very good golfer. He putts the ball very well. He's strong and has a keen interest in the game. His swing is pretty good, and he has a lot of determination to be a good player."

ARNOLD PALMER

"Of all the perks of office, the one I've enjoyed most is playing eighteen holes of golf with Arnold Palmer."

BILL CLINTON,
forty-second President of the United States

Johnny Rutherford

It was my first victory at Indianapolis, and it was incredible. Just absolutely so fulfilling. That was the job we went to do. It was one of those things where you can't really believe it. It was the perfect end to the perfect day.

You're just so caught up in the excitement of Victory Lane . . . it's something that you realize only once in a career. I've been fortunate enough to have done it three times, but the first one . . . that's the one you never forget. When that checkered flag drops and they've got that number one board up and you flash under that flag, you don't celebrate, you keep going. I always run another lap at speed just in case the scoring is wrong.

When I cross the finish line the second time, I've had a full lap to think, "Hey, I've just won this thing. I'm the winner. I've run the farthest. My God, what might they find that would penalize me, that would take the victory away. Now, what did I do. I didn't pass anybody on the yellow, I didn't . . . "And you start through the list and you start summarizing the race and thinking back, "I did this, I did . . . no they can't do anything for that, there were no pit infractions."

It's when you get the white flag signaling there's one lap to go that you really start feeling the car. It's the first time you've settled down and felt every little quiver and twitch and growl and hit and buzz and switch in that thing. You start to wonder if it's going to make it around the track.

Another aspect of this whole thing is that when you do win, you have to watch out, because for some winners, the pomp and pageantry, Victory Lane, press conferences, newspaper interviews, television interviews, the glitz and the glitter is so blinding that they lose track of what got them there.

That's why so often you see a winner of a race, particularly at Indianapolis, come up the next year and not be able to buy one, because he gets so enamored with the press clippings that he forgets all of the hard work that it takes to stay there.

That was the one thing I was always aware of . . . why I had such a long string of success. My first thought after I started winning races was, "Well, we did what we came here to do today. Let's get ready for next week." And you start preparing immediately for the next week, mentally. What has happened has happened. Let's go on to the future.

JOHNNY "LONE STAR J.R." RUTHERFORD, three-time Indy 500 champion, plus twenty-seven CART wins

"You've got to have the world's worst case of the want-to's."

JOHNNY RUTHERFORD

You don't ever think about being killed. You never really think about that. In fact, you never think you're going to crash, until you do. Sometimes you just have some painful sheet time and other times you just don't have to worry about it.

People always ask, "Aren't you ever scared out there?" I like to term it a healthy respect. You know what's there and what can happen, you just try to do everything in your experience and power to not let it happen.

Of course, now, with the cars going as fast as they go, mechanical failure is absolutely the scariest thing in the world because you're traveling at over 200 miles per hour and if something breaks that throws the car totally out of control, all you can do is hang on until it stops.

The cars are much safer now than they have ever been, and that's the beautiful part of it. You're fairly well cocooned and if you're not really hit square on, you've got a pretty good chance of surviving.

It all unfolds so quickly running at those speeds. I thought I had the perfect situation at Phoenix. I went around the outside of Dennis Firestone and had plenty of room, I was at speed, and I thought my closing rate was such that I was past him.

He just came up into me, and his right front touched my left rear and spun me. The car spun around, hit the left rear corner on the fence, bounced off, and turned around with the nose pointing toward the fence. The left rear wheel broke off and acted like a log roll, the wheel went under the car, rolled up on it and turned it up in the air. The car just kind of hung there upside down, and then it fell straight down and slid off the track. It could have just as easily been over right then and there.

It happened so quickly. It was jostling me so hard that I don't have a visual image of any of this. I don't know whether my eyes automatically clammed shut or whether it was a reflex, or if the car was throwing me around so violently with its gyrations and G forces from changing attitudes so quickly that I blacked out.

I didn't know until I saw the films that I was upside down. I was pinned under the car pretty hard, and the asphalt rubbed through my helmet as I scraped along. I was unconscious, probably from the impact when I hit. The helmet, literally, saved my life. It did more than it was designed to do. When they turned the car over, I jostled around and it must have jarred me back to consciousness. I was kind of fading in and out, and then things started coming clearer and clearer and clearer.

I was aware of all the emergency crews and the people and they were yelling and screaming and trying to see if I was alive or if I had any serious problems. They wanted to cut the car open to get me out, and I could hear Steve Edwards yelling, "Get me the jaws of life." And I said, "Steve," and everybody was yelling and he couldn't hear me and finally I yelled loud enough, "Steve!"

He made everybody shut up, and he bent down, and I said, "I'm okay, my legs are fine," and I kicked them around in the foot box, and he looked and said, "Oh. Okay." I said, "Just lift me out of this thing. I'm okay, the thing landed on my head. Just get me out of here." I can still hear his voice saying, "Oh. Oh, gosh, okay."

"Failure is not an option."

GENE KRANZ,
flight director for NASA's ill-fated Apollo 13 mission

*"Sometimes you just have a bad day. Other
people in other lines of work can have a bad day
without ending up in the hospital. They just get
up the next morning, have a cup of coffee, and
go back to work."*

JOHNNY RUTHERFORD

*"Only by pushing beyond our limits can we
really learn something new about ourselves."*

BORGE OUSLAND,
the first person to conquer both the North and South Poles —
alone and without support

Charlie Jones

I learned about fear two weeks before the 1980 Olympic Winter Games in Lake Placid, New York, when I covered the Olympic Trials of the Two-Man Bobsled.

We were in our production meeting at the Hilton Hotel when our producer, Sean McManus (now president at CBS Sports), came up with the idea that for the opening of the show I should go down the Bob Run. I immediately agreed, with the stipulation that it would definitely be in the show. There was no way in the world I was going to go through this trauma-producing exploit and then, for some reason, have the videotape left on the editing room floor.

Sean agreed and we headed out to the mountain. That's when it dawned on me that I had never actually seen a live bobsled run. I was beginning to wonder just what I'd gotten myself into.

We went through the preparations, setting the cameras, deciding exactly how it was going to be covered, and then I climbed into the back of the sled. We did not have the typical running start because if we had the typical running start there was no guarantee that I would be able to jump inside the sled, and that wouldn't look too good with the sled going down the run and me sliding along behind it!

We started from a dead stop but had no problem gathering speed. I was miked so we could capture the actual sounds, plus my commentary. I found out later that when I talked my way through the "S" turns, they had to make an edit, taking out a "Shiiiiiiiiiiiiiiiiiiiiiiiiiiiiiiiiiiiiiiiiiiiiiiiit!" which covered some six feet of audio tape.

Most vividly I remember going into the final turn. We rode high up on the ice and pulled about four G's coming out as we headed for the finish line. That high-banking turn was a huge white sheet of ice, and I had nightmares for the next five nights, waking up in a cold sweat at the sight of myself staring into frozen space.

I had a death grip on the two handles on the inside of the bobsled, when suddenly I remembered I was the brakeman. It was my job to let go of the side handles, grab the brake handles and pull them up very gently, very gradually, so the brakes, a series of metal teeth, would slowly dig into the ice, stopping the bobsled, and we would come to a halt right where the cameras were positioned just past the finish line.

My driver started screaming about the time we passed the finish line, "Brakes, Brakes." Then he screamed again, "BRAKES . . . NOW," and I shouted, "I CAN'T FIND THEM," because as I looked down the bottom of my goggles blocked out where the handles were. However, since we were about to fly off into the woods, I closed my eyes, let go of one set of handles, grabbed for the other set, and jerked as hard as I could. We rode up on the nose of the sled with a high rooster tail of ice and snow airborne about twenty feet above us as we came to a screeching halt.

It was at this moment that I heard the first critique of my debut as a bobsled brakeman: "You idiot! We're lucky you didn't get us killed."

Charlie Jones

You don't normally think of sportscasting as a dangerous profession, but sometimes your broadcasting partner can change that equation.

One Sunday in the 1960s George Ratterman and I were scheduled to broadcast a Raiders football game in Oakland's Frank Youell Field, a small, intimate stadium that was interestingly named for an undertaker. It held about 20,000 fans and had a temporary wooden press box. But, it was not a bad place to announce a game.

We were staying at the Hilton Hotel in San Francisco, and at the production meeting on Saturday afternoon there was a phone call for George. Usually at a production meeting you don't hold things up; you tell whoever's calling that you'll call back. But George got on the phone and there were a lot of "ohs," "yeahs," and "reallys." It went on for almost thirty minutes. I mean it was a really long phone call.

Now I should tell you that recently George had successfully run for sheriff of Covington, Kentucky, which is just across the river from Cincinnati. At that time Covington was the second largest (after Las Vegas) layoff betting center in the United States. George had run on the Reform ticket and had promised to clean up Covington by getting rid of all the mobsters.

The next morning when we were driving out to the stadium, I remembered his lengthy telephone conversation.

"George, what was that phone call all about?"

"Oh, it was from the FBI. It wasn't anything."

"What do you mean, it wasn't anything, it was from the FBI! It had to be something. What did the FBI want?"

"Well, it was the FBI in San Francisco, and they got a call from the FBI in Cincinnati. They were told that a contract had been put out on my life, and that a sniper was going to try and assassinate me during today's game."

"GEORGE, DO THEY KNOW WHAT YOU LOOK LIKE?"

Now, try sitting in an open wooden press box next to a broadcast partner who's on somebody's hit list. The booth was like a shack. A bullet could have found us from any side. There were a lot of tall buildings all around, and a sniper could have been hiding anywhere. I'm not kidding when I tell you I spent the entire ball game leaning as far away from George as I possibly could.

What I really wanted was a big sign with an arrow on it saying: "THAT'S RATTERMAN OVER THERE."

But there wasn't an attempt on anyone's life that day. I'm still here and so is George, who now resides in Denver where, I suspect, he remains threatened only by the winter snows.

*"Success is doing what it takes
in spite of one's fear."*

JOHNNY RUTHERFORD

Chris Evert

I think if you look at most athletes who've been champions over a long period of time, you'll see they possess tunnel vision.

For them to be a better human being or a more well rounded human being, what they have to do is learn to turn it on and off. If they can do that, they've got the best of both worlds.

But there are some who can't. I always found it hard to do. It's that hunger, that desire. It isn't the money. That's the funny thing. It's pride and maybe even ego.

CHRIS EVERT won at least one Grand Slam singles title every year from 1974 to 1986. She ranks second in all-time tournament victories (157).

"Single-mindedness.
I hate to say it because I don't think
it's the best thing for developing a person,
but the single-mindedness —
just concentrating in that one area —
that's what it takes to be a champion."

CHRIS EVERT

Steve Lundquist

Winning is like Christmas Day for kids. Your joy is incredible, obviously, but Christmas Day for kids is from October on, when kids start saying, "Christmas, Christmas, Christmas." November comes: "Christmas, Christmas, Christmas." December: "Christmas, Christmas, Christmas." You get a week out and it's "Christmas, Christmas, Christmas." Christmas Eve and they're just going nuts.

Christmas morning, they wake up and they open their presents, and by eight in the morning they're already playing with them. By the afternoon they're saying, "Is that it?"

All this hype for three months.

Only for me it was fifteen years, training fifteen years for that one minute and one second and the gold medal. I said, "Wow, that was it?" There's a little emptiness. I don't know how to describe that.

STEVE LUNDQUIST, two-time gold medalist swimmer at the 1984 Olympics.

"Like Scarlett O'Hara said,
tomorrow's another day.
But in the Olympics,
tomorrow is four years away."

MICHAEL O'BRIEN,
gold medal winner in the 1984 Los Angeles Olympics,
swimming the 1500-meters.

Talking winning with Jack Nicklaus in 1965

Interviewing Lee Trevino following his victory at the Hawaiian
Open in 1968

With Bob Trumpy, Charlie's current broadcast partner and Pro-Bowl tight end for the Cincinnati Bengals

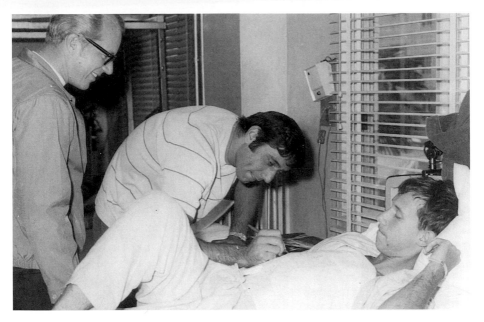

Following the New York Jets' Super Bowl III huge upset victory, Charlie joined their quarterback, Joe Namath, on a USO tour of hospitals in the Far East.

With more than twenty-five years of managerial experience, Sparky Anderson may know all there is to know about winning.

Hitting the links with former Lakers superstar Earvin "Magic" Johnson

Taking a break from broadcasting with golf great Johnny Miller during the 1991 Ryder Cup in Kiawah Island, South Carolina

With Todd Christensen, former broadcast partner and Pro-Bowl tight end for the Raiders

Chatting with former broadcast partner and Olympic Decathlete Bruce Jenner

Charlie Jones and Carl Lewis, emphasizing his having won
four gold medals in the Los Angeles Olympics and his attempt
to win four more at Seoul

On track with Olympic gold medalist Frank Shorter and Missy
Kane, track coach at the University of Tennessee

Charlie today, with former partner Randy Cross, former offensive lineman for the three-time Super Bowl champion 49ers

Peter Carruthers

The evening of the Olympic long program came, and Kitty and I had never felt so determined to turn in a great performance as we had that evening, and I don't think we've felt that way since. There had been so much hard work that had gone into this competition that we felt, "This is it. This is the right time for us."

When Kitty and I started our program, we looked into each other's eyes and there was so much intensity, I just can't begin to describe it. We continued from that point and skated above ourselves, better than we ever thought we could.

There was one moment that was really special to me. It was when we were in our pair sit spin, spinning around, about three quarters of the way through the long program. When we came up to finish the spin, there was a pause in the music just before our final moments in the program. We both looked up and "presented to the music," and I remember seeing the Olympic rings. It was pretty incredible. That moment froze for me, because for some reason there were Olympic rings hanging right over us. I saw those rings and I thought, "Boy, we're doing it. Hold on. Just stand up for the rest of the program."

And when it ended, all I could remember was that I just . . . I just felt that was our night.

When we finished, we hugged and embraced, and at that point, I don't think we cared what place we were going to finish, what anybody was thinking, it was just that Kitty and I had succeeded as a team together in one of the most difficult pressure situations we'd ever faced. We hugged and embraced and finally we came back to reality and took our bow and got off the ice.

Our life changed from that point on, and we haven't looked back. We left the building that evening different people. We were completely elated.

Kitty and I are family. We're brother and sister. We kept it right in the family. There were now two Olympic medals within the Carruthers family. It was very special. It was a complete family effort. I don't know if many families get to experience things like that.

PETER AND KITTY CARRUTHERS, the brother and sister figure skating team, were U. S. champions for four years consecutively (1980–84) and were silver medalists at the 1984 Sarajevo Olympics.

"When that Olympic silver medal went around my neck, I'd never felt something that heavy. It was an incredible feeling. When I touched it and looked at it, it glowed back at me."

PETER CARRUTHERS

"You can attain any goal if you put your mind to it."

KITTY CARRUTHERS

Charlie Jones

On February 20, 1980, a date that everybody might not remember but one which sticks so vividly in my mind, I arrived with John Gonzalez, our producer-director, in Moscow on our way to cover the World Championships of Motorcycle Racing on Ice in Kalinin, in the Soviet Union.

After almost three hours of working our way through passport control and customs, when we were finally in the city of Moscow, I asked our Russian representative, Vladimir Eggar, "Are they out?" He said, "They're out of everything." I said, "No, are the Soviets out of Afghanistan?" He said, "You've got to be kidding."

You see, February 20, 1980, was the deadline President Jimmy Carter had set for the boycott of the Moscow Olympic Games so I knew at that moment we would not be coming back in the summer.

This had a devastating effect on me because I was scheduled to host both Track and Field and Gymnastics, two of the premier events. But more than that, it had a devastating effect on those American athletes who only had that small window of time in which to compete in their sport at the Olympic level.

Bart Conner, the gymnast, was one of those athletes. But Bart wanted to stretch his vision, so he immediately started his preparation for the 1984 Games in Los Angeles.

At that time NBC was covering gymnastics throughout the world, and Bart would join us in various cities such as Budapest or Bucharest or London as our color analyst.

He is one of those special athletes, a young man who lights up a room when he walks in, but age was starting to catch up to him as he continued to prepare for the '84 Games.

Seven months before the Los Angeles Games, Bart was in Nagoya, Japan, competing in the Cunichi Cup when disaster struck. He tore the tendon from his left biceps, which is a debilitating injury to a gymnast, particularly to one whose premier event is the parallel bars.

Bart immediately got on a plane and flew to Las Vegas where he had surgery (they drilled a hole in his shoulder, drew the tendon through the hole, and then stapled it to the bone) and quickly started his rehabilitation. Then, just little by little, day by day, and week by week, Bart fought his way back.

There were two U. S. gymnastic trials in 1984. In the first trial he fell, immediately withdrew and filed an injury report, which meant that he put all his chances of making the Olympic team on the second trial. The strategy worked as Bart was the last man to make the squad, by three-tenths of a point. He then went on to win two gold medals in the Los Angeles Games.

About a week afterwards, I asked Bart how in the world was he able to overcome the injury, come back after the surgery, go through all the rehabilitation and then make the Olympic team and win two gold medals? Bart said, "Well, it was the way that I was raised. And in all honesty I have to give the credit to my parents."

I said, "That's well and good," because all athletes, when they reach the pinnacle of success, have the tendency to say that same thing.

Bart said, "No. No, it was entirely different with me. As

long as I can remember, every night when I went to bed, either my mother or my father sat with me and asked, 'What did you do today that was a success?' As a kid, maybe it was a crayon drawing, or perhaps as I got a little older it was A-B-C, not the whole alphabet but just the first three letters, A-B-C, or maybe it was when I was a little bit older and did my first back flip off the living room couch but every night we would always review the day and pick out one thing in which I was successful. So every night of my life I have gone to bed a successful man.

"I used this technique when I was going through my rehabilitation. I would go back through the day and find one thing, one small improvement, one small step, one small triumph, and I would remind myself of that as I went to sleep. So every night I continued to go to sleep a successful man."

What a great lesson that is, because all of us, every day, have our successes. We just need to remind ourselves of that fact and then take them to sleep with us every night, as a successful person.

"The people we admire in our lives
are ordinary people that have been able
to accomplish some extraordinary things.
The things that make them extraordinary
are things that we all possess."

ROLF BENIRSCHKE,
San Diego Chargers' placekicker from 1977 to 1986, once held
the Charger record for most career points (766).

"The Olympic medal is nice, but the title is more important. You can't carry the medal around. You can't display it, because if someone breaks into your house that's the first thing they'll steal. You can't put it in a safe-deposit box, because you have to go over to the bank if you want to show it to anyone. I keep mine in a sock."

MARK LENZI,
1992 Olympic springboard champion

"She is just a little girl who was never the roughest girl. . . . Always a little shy, always standing behind someone else. But sometimes this is the person with the biggest ggrrrr."

BELA KAROLYI,
Olympic gymnastic coach, speaking about Keri Strug, who indelibly etched herself into Olympic history by sticking her final vault while suffering from a sprained ankle, leading the U.S. to its first ever gold medal in the women's team event.

Chris Marlowe

This happened in the locker room at the Long Beach Arena as the United States Men's Volleyball team was set to take the floor against Brazil for the gold medal in the 1984 Olympic Games.

We're all sitting around, and our assistant coach, Bill Neville, had just given us a speech about how important it is to go out and play well in this match in front of eighty million people. Then our head coach, Doug Beal, had gotten up and talked about the parameters of the game—you need to pass, you need to set—and basically we were just about asleep by then, when all of a sudden, out of nowhere, appears Tom Selleck.

Now this wasn't unusual, simply because Tom Selleck was the Honorary Captain of the Men's Olympic Volleyball team, so we had seen him before, but he had never been in the locker room. I looked around at the rest of the players and Karch Karaly, our best player, was lost in thought, Pat Bowers was shoveling in Jujubees, Steve Timmons was in the process of moussing his hair, and Alois Berzins was reading a book.

But when Selleck got up to speak, everybody took notice and it became very quiet. The first thing Selleck said was, "All my life I've been an athlete. I went to USC, I played there. In my heart I'm an athlete. I've received a lot of notoriety as Magnum, a lot of publicity, but as an athlete, I would give anything in the world to be in your shoes right now."

As he said that, you could almost hear a pin drop. And

91

then he continued, "I've received a lot of recognition in my time, I've been nominated for honors, I've gone to the Academy Awards, I've met all kinds of people, but the greatest honor I've ever had is to be with you guys right now, before you go out and go for the gold." And when he said that, that was the end of his speech but no one knew, and we're all sitting there very quietly.

Then, as captain of the team, I jumped up and shouted, "Well, if it's good enough for Magnum, then it's good enough for the USA. Let's get out there." We ran out and we kicked the crap out of Brazil . . . and the rest is history.

CHRIS MARLOWE, captain, 1984 U. S. Olympic Men's Volleyball Team and current NBC and ESPN sportscaster.

"It's all about winning.
That's what people
remember the most."

DON BAYLOR

Charlie Jones

One of the most exciting events I've ever broadcast was the World Cup of Soccer in Mexico in 1986. This was to be the most watched worldwide sports event in television history, but unfortunately NBC's coverage was going to lose some $5 million, so we were treated like the proverbial stepchild.

There were thirteen of us (we dubbed ourselves the Dirty Thirteen) in Mexico for the five weeks of the event. A "good luck" telegram from our executive producer, Mike Weisman, before the opening weekend was the first and last message we received from the home office in New York City.

We televised the opening game from Azteca Stadium in Mexico City, and then the next day we were scheduled to broadcast the Sunday contest between Spain and Brazil, two of the top contenders, in Guadalajara.

After the Saturday event, we jumped into our rented van and headed for the airport. With the traffic it was difficult to get there but we still arrived in the time for our flight. However when we checked in with AeroMexico, we discovered a formidable problem. Our flight to Guadalajara had been oversold. I mean *really* oversold . . . by 128 seats!

Our producer-director, John Gonzalez, immediately sat down and figured out that by cutting all corners we could get on the air, bare bones, the next day in Guadalajara with just seven people. Gonzo, who speaks fluent Spanish, then went to work. With his great smile and with big doses of flattery and guile, he was able to wheedle seven tickets, so we said farewell to our companions and boarded Flight 126 for Guadalajara.

The plane was filled with Spanish fans, and they were in high spirits, leading yells and shouting team cheers. I was sitting on the aisle in the fifth row when they started, of all things, the "wave." As it reached the front of the plane, the cockpit door was open, and both the pilot and copilot raised their arms continuing the "wave," which did not fill me with great confidence in their flying ability, but we did finally arrive safely in Guadalajara.

The next morning we were to meet in the hotel lobby at seven o'clock, and as I came down the glass-enclosed elevator in the atrium, I looked down, and there below were the other six members of the Dirty Thirteen. In my mind the only way they could have gotten here was to drive the rented van over the mountains on that treacherous, winding, two-lane highway through the back country of Mexico. A very dangerous drive, just to be with us for the Sunday telecast. Wow! Now that's teamwork!

As I got off the elevator and greeted everyone, I said, "When in the world did you arrive?" They replied, "Oh, about eight o'clock last night." I said, "Eight o'clock last night! You got here at eight o'clock last night?"

Therein lies the tale. One of the remaining members of the Dirty Thirteen was Art Durazo, who also speaks perfect Spanish. Art noticed that posted on the AeroMexico Departure Board was a flight to Ciudad Obregon. Art knew that Ciudad Obregon is directly north of Guadalajara, so he went about gathering six boarding passes for that flight. After taking off, Art lavishly passed out NBC Sports caps and NBC soccer pins to the pilot, copilot, flight engineer, and the entire cabin crew, and, in the process, told them of their plight. The flight crew then decided they would come to the rescue.

So, AeroMexico Flight 420, bound for Ciudad Obregon, made an unscheduled landing in Guadalajara. The steps swung down, our intrepid crew got off the plane, the steps were pulled back up, the door closed, they waved goodbye to their newfound friends, the flight was off, and the Dirty Thirteen were together again in Guadalajara.

"To be average
scares the hell out of me."

DICK SEEGER,
author of *I've Been Thinking*, among other inspirational books

"Believe the unbelievable."

MARY LOU RETTON
was the first American to ever win the gold medal in Individual All-Around gymnastics. She won it in the 1984 L.A. Olympics, sealing the medal with a perfect ten on the vault.

Charlie Jones

The reason this book contains so many quotations is that I've always been fascinated by them. Over the years I've collected quotes from newspapers, books, magazines, and from my interviews. I have them hanging in my office, stuffed in filing cabinets, in my billfold, on the nightstand, and in my garage, where I see them every time I get in and out of my car.

But my all-time favorite sports quote just didn't fit anywhere in the book:

*"I always eat frog legs before I pitch.
It makes my fastball jump."*

RICK RICE,
journeyman minor league pitcher, circa 1920

THE EDGE

It seems as if everyone in every walk of life is constantly looking for The Edge. *I know that I am.* The Edge *establishes an advantage, which leads to confidence, which hopefully leads to victory.*

I've discovered The Edge *comes in many forms. Sometimes you are born with it (a member of the lucky gene club), sometimes you inherit it (from the people you interact with), and other times hard work brings it to you (but not as often as you would like).*

However, The Edge *is really just a case of mental gymnastics, because if you feel you have* The Edge, *then in reality, you do.*

Todd Christensen

I was in the Pro Bowl in Hawaii with Steve Largent. The NFC had punted and we had the ball for the first time on about our ten-yard line. We went out there and all of a sudden, Largent comes running into the huddle, and he's all excited. I said, "What, what is it?"

He said, "Listen to this. Now look down. The grains of the Astroturf are running east and west, which means that in the first quarter we'll be fast but not quick, and in the second quarter, quick but not fast. So the first quarter we should be running the ups and the deep patterns, and the second quarter a shorter route because we'll be able to cut better."

The grains of the Astroturf running east and west? I mean, are you kidding me? This is the Pro Bowl, for god's sake, and I laughed. Then it dawned on me this is what makes Largent so great, because, who cares? The huddle is filled with the breath of Mai Tais and here's this guy, a twelve-year veteran, nine million records, greatest receiver of all time, and he comes in all excited to tell me that the grains of the Astroturf are running east to west.

I was embarrassed because I'm one of those guys who always took pride in the fact that I've got an edge. I mean, this is a no-brainer game, and Largent was like this. Unbelievable.

"I play the game hard. I get offended when people don't do the same. That bothers me. It bothers me a lot. I'm trying to do my best to get to a certain point, and if one of my teammates is taking away my opportunity, I'm going to confront him."

ERIC KARROS,
Los Angeles Dodger first baseman

"Work never bothers me like it bothers some people. You can outwork the best player in the world."

BEN HOGAN
has been recognized as one of the greatest golfers in history. His wins included four U.S. Opens, two Masters, two PGA Championships, and a British Open.

Todd Christensen

After practice on Thursdays I'd always have somebody throw me the ball and I'd one-hand catch it, standing still. The reason is that when you see players making those great one-handed catches in a game, they're running with the ball, and that cushions the ball because they have their momentum going in the same direction.

If you can stand still and catch it with one hand, when all you have to brace it against is your hand, then you have that incredible tactile sensation of catching the ball.

I would stand ten yards away and I would one-hand catch, because every other one-hand catch I'd make would be when I'd be running an in, an out, a post, running with the ball so I could cushion it, which made it that much easier to one-hand catch.

Nobody else ever believed in that. I did. I was a big believer in that. So I would always do that on Thursdays.

"Don't let anyone else's opinion of you get you down, because the only opinion that counts is yours. No one can take that away from you."

TERRY BRADSHAW

Bill Walsh

The first thing to remember is that your mind can really affect your ability to perform. It's almost a serene, purist state of mind you get in when you're competing with full, ultimate confidence, poise, self-assurance, and preparation. I think the mind-set is what an athlete needs in order to be at his best, whether he finishes first or last, to be able to perform without any negative connotations to your thoughts.

It's the negatives that you don't want to cross your mind. The apprehension about whether you're good enough, whether you're really prepared, or the fear that your opponent is simply better than you are. When fatigue sets in, your mind begins to play crazy tricks on you.

You must train yourself to cut through all that. Much of it is how long and how hard you prepared, and also just how good you've become, and whether you've really been willing to totally commit yourself over a period of time.

The positive side is pretty simple. The negative forces come from all angles. They can be personal, they can be physical, they can be an apprehension about your opponent, they can be the absolute fear that crosses your mind when you feel fatigue setting in. Those are the things that the athlete can overcome only if he's fully prepared and has developed a positive state of mind about his skills.

BILL WALSH, head coach of the San Francisco 49ers, led the team to three Super Bowl wins (1982, 1985, 1989). He has also had an exceptional career as the head football coach at Stanford University, as well as an NBC broadcaster.

*"I think the Super Bowl is usually a
disappointment because of the way football
players train. They don't train to peak at the
Super Bowl because if you think about it, they
don't even know if they're going to be there until
two weeks before."*

FRANK SHORTER,
Olympic Marathon gold medalist in 1972, became the first
American since 1908 to win the event.

*"I think the edge
is not being afraid of the situation.
It should never cross your mind
that it can't be done."*

JOHN ELWAY,
quarterback of the Denver Broncos since 1983 and future Hall of
Famer, is famous for his last-minute game-winning drives.

*"I'd rather get beat up and win
than not get beat up and lose."*

JOHN ELWAY

Johnny Rutherford

Always before the Indy 500 the local newspaper comes out with a picture and the speeds of each driver in the field, and how all thirty-three line up. Then the night before the race I like to sit down and see where I'm starting and look at the drivers around me and try to figure scenarios.

This guy's going to be charging, that guy is not going to be pushing as hard. And I visualize different situations: where he will go, what he will do, whether I can pressure him, whether he's the one that I've got to be careful of, how I can move up through the field. Then at the start of the race that all goes out the window.

"You can map out a fight plan or a life plan, but when the action starts, it may not go the way you planned, and you're down to your reflexes – which means your training. That's where your roadwork shows. If you cheated on that in the dark of morning – well, you're getting found out now, under the bright lights."

JOE FRAZIER,
heavyweight boxing champ from 1970 to 1973, is perhaps best-known for his three epic bouts with Muhammad Ali.

Bruce Jenner

Fear is part of the process. If you weren't scared, you'd be in trouble. I was scared to death, but I made fear score points for me. Fear is right behind me, fear is six inches off my back, that's where fear is. And it's there, it's present, and I can feel its presence.

It's not going to catch me. When I'm running, fear is right behind me, and I'm not going to let it catch me. I'm going to take fear and use it to my advantage. It's going to make me run scared. But I won't let it catch up to me. I won't let it get in front of me; if I did, it would slow me down, it could even make me stop.

BRUCE JENNER set the world decathlon record in winning the gold medal at the 1976 Montreal Olympics.

"Fear makes some guys call in sick or be tentative. Dennis Eckersley uses fear to get him ready for every stinking time he pitches."

TONY LaRUSSA

Bruce Jenner

Don't come near me, because I've got other things on my mind. Family, friends, relatives, don't come near me. That was my mind-set for the Montreal Olympics in 1976. I was hard to live with for a long time, especially those last few months because I'd just spent twelve years of my life preparing for these two days of competition. This is not fun, this is not fun and games. This is business. This is getting down to it.

I was extremely intense, very uptight. My mind was working overtime. Scared to death. I just wanted to get this thing over with. All those feelings went through my mind. But I was extremely confident also. In my case, I was the favorite. I had beaten everybody who was there. To be honest with you, I really couldn't see myself losing, unless I really screwed up. Every night when I went to sleep I saw myself winning.

I saw myself coming off the final turn, still in the turn, not on the straightaway yet, running that final turn in the 1500 meters. I've got the gold medal jingling in my back pocket. I can hear it jingling. Jingle, jingle, jingle. And I'm running that turn. I sort of lean into that turn. I'm running that baby, then as I come off the turn, I straighten and I look down that straightaway, about 100 meters to the finish line, and I'm looking at the finish line thinking, "All I've got to do is run from here to there, to be the Olympic champion." Simple.

That was the dream I had, the final turn in the 1500 meters. That's what I thought about. I could feel myself being there.

When I was actually at that moment in the Olympics I

felt like stopping. I felt like holding on to that moment. I didn't stop physically. Physically I continued to run real hard. But mentally I stopped, I looked around. I actually physically looked around. I looked at the stadium, I looked at the bleachers, I looked at the people in the stands.

I can remember looking up and everybody was standing and applauding. I remember looking to the infield quickly. I kept thinking to myself, "Hold on to this moment. It's going to be over in a second. Hold on to it." So I was going, "Click, now I know what that looks like. Okay, look over there, click. Now take a picture over here, click. Hold on to that." Mental snapshots.

See, I was in a different position. It wasn't like I was trying, at that point, to win my medal. I already knew I had it. I wanted to score 6,800 points, so I had to run a hard 1500 meters. I thought, "What the heck, I've got fifty, sixty years to recuperate. Might as well go for it, huh?" So, I could enjoy that 1500 meters a little bit more because I just had to run a great time, that's all. I knew I was ready to do that. But there was no major pressure on me at that point.

For me, the pressure was leading up to the Games. Until I got going. Until I ran the 100 meters, the first event. I ran a very good time for me, and compared to the other guys who were running, my time was much better than what they did. So I was ahead of them already. That was a great start. And then I felt the pressure the next morning, with the hurdles, because I had had such an outstanding first day.

The night between events I slept terribly. It was raining outside all night long. The next day was the hurdles on a wet track, the pole vault on a wet runway, not good. Here I've got five great events going for me the first day, and it could rain the second day.

My heart was pounding so hard the sheets were

bouncing off my chest. It rained all night, pouring rain, so I couldn't get any sleep. I'm right in the middle of the biggest meet of my life and I'm supposed to sleep? Forget it, it doesn't work. I only slept for about three hours. But, when I woke up, I was wide awake. Absolutely wide awake. It was like I never slept. My eyes opened up, I got out of bed, put my stuff on, went down, got breakfast and went to work.

I learned a long time ago that the night in between decathlon events I'm not going to sleep very well, so the week before I tried to get more sleep than I would normally get. I loaded up on sleep. The biggest problem you can have is to lie there, not being able to sleep and thinking, "I've got to get some sleep or I'm not going to be able to run well tomorrow."

Even at that, it's tough to sleep the week before, but I would load up as much as I could, so I had at least a clear conscience that I could stay up all night if I had to. And I'd be able to go out the second day and still be fresh as a daisy.

I was extremely focused both days. I didn't really care if there was another human being there watching. I didn't care if there was a TV camera. You have a lot of time in between events where you sit and you wait for the next event or you're warming up, and you certainly are aware of where you're at, but I can't remember any time in the competition that I heard the crowd noise, except maybe in the 1500 meters, going down the backstretch.

That was the only time I noticed, "Man, it's loud in here." Because at that time the pressure was off, I was just running a good time, so I was a little bit more aware of what was going on around me. Up to that point, no. Any time I was competing I really never considered the audience or where I was. It was between me and that little track, that little vaulting pole, and that little discus. That was the competition.

"When you go to the Olympic Games, you're taking on the rest of the world, in front of the entire world."

BRUCE JENNER

"Competition is more inward than it is outward."

BRUCE JENNER

"It's all about the journey, not the outcome."

CARL LEWIS

Charlie Jones

As a broadcaster, I've found there are all kinds of pressures and all kinds of ways to deal with pressure. One of the most interesting was told to me by Vin Scully, the legendary Dodger broadcaster.

The year was 1955 and the Dodgers and the Yankees were playing in the seventh game of the World Series. Vin was still living at home in New York and was broadcasting the game on radio. Naturally, his mother was listening.

In this series the Yankees had won the first two games, the Dodgers came back to win three in a row, then the Yankees won game six, thus setting the scene for the seventh game. Keep in mind that the Yankees had won every World Series in which they had faced the Brooklyn Dodgers: '41, '47, '49, '52, and '53. So, if you were a Dodger fan there was a lot to be nervous about.

As the first inning got underway on the radio, Vin's mother began to feel the pressure. To quiet her nerves she got out the leash, found their dog Blackie, and took him for a walk around the block. By the time she returned home, the first inning was over, she had calmed down and was now ready to listen to the second inning.

Suddenly it became nervous time again so she got the leash, found Blackie, and they walked around the block again.

This game was a classic nail-biter, and Vin's mother felt the same anxiety in every inning. Each time she came up with the same solution, walk Blackie around the block.

Finally, the pressure-packed ninth inning arrived, with

Johnny Podres shutting out the Yankees 2-0. The scene was
set for the Dodgers to finally win their first World Series
against the Yankees.

Vin's mother couldn't stand it any longer, so she got the
leash and went looking for Blackie. But he had disappeared.
She searched all over the house and when she finally found
him, Blackie was in the back of the closet hiding behind
the shoe boxes, totally exhausted.

*"I look at the World Series
as an opportunity to raise my game
to another level."*

JOHN SMOLTZ,
Atlanta Braves pitcher, from 1988 to the present, was the 1996
Cy Young Award winner with a 24-8 record and 2.94 ERA.

*"It's indescribable. It's like an addiction, this
intensity to reach a higher level. My mind won't
allow me to rest. It would be so easy to say, 'Hey,
I had three pretty good years. I should relax a
little, think about all I've accomplished.' But I
can't do it . . . I just can't do it. It's a fear of
failure. When it's over, I want to say, 'Hey, I had
a pretty good run. I gave it all I had.' But until
that day, I'll never, ever be satisfied."*

MIKE PIAZZA,
Los Angeles Dodger catcher, has hit more home runs (91) in his
first three seasons than any catcher in baseball history.

Bill Walton

Coach John Wooden taught us about visualization, about seeing the game happen. When you're a basketball player you have a lot of time where you just sit around and think. You think about the game that's coming up and how you're going to play.

By game time I'd already seen the whole game ten times over, exactly what was going to happen, like a video that I was part of, where I would see the ball and I'd see opponents driving at me, or I'd see teammates wide open who I'd be passing to, or I'd see how a center was going to guard me. I'd see his shots so I'd know how to go for the rebound, or how I was going to cut a guy off if he was penetrating. I'd seen it all before.

"I put a lot of effort and thought into how I was going to win games."

BILL WALTON

112

Bart Conner

I look at it from two perspectives when I mentally rehearse my routines. First, I'm the gymnast who's doing the routine, and if I'm on the high bar, I feel my body going through the motions. I feel the bottom of the swing. I feel the rhythm and the timing. I feel where it speeds up and where it slows down.

Then I try to visualize as if I were the person who was standing back and watching me perform, and that's a little different picture. I was always at my best when I saw that picture. It's like once you had visualized it, you see the scene, you see the gym, you see the judges, you see the arena, you see where the equipment is, you see where the chalk tray is, you see everything. So when you actually go to perform, it's like, "Oh, I've been here before." Then you have such confidence because it's like you've already been through this.

I have to admit that sometimes visualizing is a little scary too, because sometimes I make mistakes when I'm visualizing my routine. I found that if I'm on the high bar and I'm doing a release move, I might pitch it out and fly off. So I have to "rewind" a little bit and pick up where I was.

I always wondered why I had those kinds of visualizations. Well, what I had been doing, and these are my own thoughts, was I had been admitting to myself, being honest, that something bad could happen.

Now I'm approaching this with a positive frame of mind, so I start; here's my first trick, here's my second trick—but I have also considered the variables. What if I'm pitching this out a little bit? Well, here's how I correct. What if I'm a little slow here? Well, here's how I correct. What if I'm short? Well, I'll just turn and go in this direction.

So what I have done then, in my mind, is see the perfect routine. I've gotten through it, but I've also seen all the possibilities, so that when I step up I have this feeling of confidence. I don't know exactly how it's going to go but I'm ready for any way that it does go.

BART CONNER won two gold medals in gymnastics at the 1984 Los Angeles Olympics.

"Intelligence doesn't enable you to succeed. Being smart does – being able to integrate a little intelligence with common sense."

ROBERT KRAFT

"The key with winning is how you handle winning."

RAY RHODES,
head coach, Philadelphia Eagles

Charlie Jones

I always visualized myself as a game show host, and several years ago I had my golden opportunity. I hosted a prime time, sports game show spoof titled *Almost Anything Goes,* where three small towns, 8,000 to 12,000 in size, played zany games against each other.

As a summer replacement on ABC, we had dynamite numbers and were picked up for the fall. However, our audience was not nearly as large during the winter, and we got canceled.

The one thing I do remember is when we were in Douglas, Arizona, shooting the Southwest Championships, the mayor held a reception for us at the small country club in town. In his welcoming speech, he said, "These are the two greatest weeks in the history of Douglas."

I was thinking, I wonder what he means by that? We've only been in town for a week. The mayor continued, "This week *Almost Anything Goes,* and last week, the Pizza Hut opened."

One day I was listening to Benny Parsons do an interview. They were talking about drivers' eyesight, and their abilities to do some things that other people can't even fathom.

Benny said, "You know, race drivers can read phonograph labels on the turntable when they're turning." And it dawned on me that I've been able to do that for years.

I can remember looking at a record turning and being able to read the name and even who performed it while it was spinning on the turntable.

You just are able to . . . it's like flash cards. You know how they hold up a card in front of you and ask how many spots are there? Drivers are very good at that, being able to determine who it was, whether it's friend or foe.

*"You have to train your mind
like you train your body."*

BRUCE JENNER

*"Do the ordinary things, in an extraordinary
way."*

GEORGE ALLEN
head coach for the Los Angeles Rams and Washington Redskins

There is no doubt in my mind that superstar athletes are different from the rest of us.

On one Fourth of July, Johnny Rutherford and I were announcing a dirt track race in Reading, Pennsylvania, for NBC's SportsWorld. That morning as Johnny was driving us to the track in our rental car, I ventured the question, "Are race car drivers really better drivers than the rest of us?"

There was a bit of method in my question as I've always perceived myself as a pretty good driver. Johnny answered, "Oh, yes, there is a big difference." I countered, "Oh, yeah?"

He immediately continued, "Charlie, you'll notice there are eight cars behind us on the freeway all going about 65 miles per hour—that's our speed, except for that red Buick, which is closing fast on our left. In front of us are four cars and the black one on the right is getting ready to change lanes. Coming in the opposite direction on the turnpike are five cars and a semi-tractor-trailer that's experiencing some problems as he's starting to slow down and pull over to his right. About a quarter of a mile away is the on-ramp, and there are three cars that will merge about the time we get there. I'm a little concerned about the third car, the white Ford. The lady that's driving it has a herky-jerky motion, and I'll be keeping my eye on her."

Johnny's right. They are better drivers than we are.

Charlie Jones

In January of 1969, immediately following Super Bowl III and the upset by the New York Jets over the Baltimore Colts, I received a phone call from NFL commissioner Pete Rozelle. Pete invited me to go on an NFL/USO tour of the military hospitals in the Far East.

I was very proud of this honor, and I joined Joe Namath, just coming off that great Super Bowl victory, Marv Fleming, then a tight end for the Green Bay Packers, Jim Otto, the future Hall of Fame center for the Oakland Raiders, and the outstanding offensive tackle for the New York Giants, Steve Wright, for the three-week trip.

My most poignant memory was when we arrived at Clark Air Force Base in the Philippines. We had flown most of the night from Okinawa, and when we stepped off the plane, we were met by USO personnel. They immediately took us to the base hospital because they wanted us to meet Andy McKinny. Andy McKinny had been in an electrical accident working on power lines in Vietnam and both his arms had been amputated at the shoulder. Among other things, he was experiencing kidney failure and was in terrible condition. They wanted us to see him immediately because they were afraid he would not be alive when we made our scheduled hospital visit that afternoon.

As Josie Morris, the USO representative at Clark, confided to me, she really felt that Andy had stayed alive because he wanted a chance to meet Joe Namath and the other NFL players.

When we went into his room, Andy had tubes running

in and out of him and was on an IV, taking in at least a quart of vodka, as Namath pointed out. It was a friendly visit, we took some pictures and had a chance to cheer him up just a little bit.

Later that afternoon, when we came back to visit the other patients in the hospital, we stuck our heads in Andy's room to say hello, and he seemed to be a little better.

The next day we were helicoptered to the other side of the Philippines, to Subic Bay, where we visited more hospitals. After three days we returned to Clark Air Force Base and when the helicopter landed, the USO people were there to meet us again and said, "You've got to come see Andy right now."

We were expecting the absolute worst, but when we walked into his room this time Andy was sitting up in bed with a big smile on his face. He had a tray table in front of him with a book holder and was turning the pages of the book with an eraser on the end of a pencil he was holding in his mouth. Andy looked like an entirely different person. The transformation in this young man in just three days was truly remarkable.

I found out later that Andy had been shipped back to Walter Reed Hospital in Washington, D.C. for further treatment and rehabilitation. That summer I was in our nation's capitol with NBC for the All-Star Baseball Game, and I had an afternoon off, so I drove out to Walter Reed Hospital to see Andy.

I walked up to the desk in the lobby, introduced myself, and said I would like to see Andy McKinny, that I understood he was there. The receptionist went through the files and said, "No, we don't have any Andy McKinny here." My heart dropped immediately, and I said, "Could you please double check?" She went back through another whole set of files in a cabinet, came back and said, "No, we don't have any records of Andy McKinny."

As I started to turn away, a sergeant came up and said, "Did I overhear you say that you were looking for Andy McKinny?" I said, "Yes, I am," and he replied, "Oh, let me tell you about Andy. He's such a neat young man. He came back and got his prothesis, his two new arms, and learned to use them faster than anyone we've ever had here. He's the nicest young man and with his outgoing personality he had friends all over the hospital. Just two weeks ago Andy was sent home to West Virginia."

I got in my rental car and drove back to the Sheraton Hotel, and believe me, I had a smile on my face that afternoon that stretched from ear to ear.

THE ZONE

The Zone *is that unique, wonderful, mysterious place which we all have visited at one time or another.*

During my broadcasting career when I was in The Zone, *it was a magical experience. There was such clarity my eyesight was 20/10. I could anticipate every play. It was as if I could read the quarterback's mind, see the game plan in front of me, and sense the pattern of the offensive coordinator's thoughts. Everything but my mouth was in slow motion. It was easy to follow the action, and I never had to reach for words to describe a play. And, because I was having so much fun, I never wanted the game to end.*

The Zone *is the perfect day. The smiles are larger, the heart is fuller, and the sunset is more beautiful. Unfortunately, we're not allowed to visit* The Zone *every day.*

Greg Norman

Everything goes by in slow motion. Your swing feels like it's in slow motion, it seems like you've got forever, timewise, to make a decision. You're at peace with yourself. You never second guess when you pull out a club. Your hand goes automatically to the right club. There's never an in-between yardage.

It's the most singular experience any athlete could ever have. I just wish everybody in the world could go through this because to be able to feel like you can do anything with a golf ball is a phenomenal experience.

It's a wonderful feeling, so unique to an athlete. I wish I could put you into my body to experience it. It's a rush. It really is a rush. When I know . . . I can say to my caddie, "What's the yardage?" And he'll say, "Exactly 183 yards." I know that I'm in my zone. And he knows too, he knows how good I'm feeling. So that will give you an idea. I can put it within a foot and half, two feet from that 183-yard mark.

*"The inner being
is what takes you to another level."*

GREG NORMAN

123

*"I've been diving on a tank of air,
and I'll stay down thirty minutes longer
than my diving partner because I've controlled
my breathing and controlled the pace of my
body and my energy level."*

GREG NORMAN

*"When I won my second U.S. Open,
I sucked up energy from my playing partner,
Greg Norman."*

HALE IRWIN

*"When you get on a roll, just let it happen. Let
the reins of the horse go and let him run as fast
as he wants to run."*

GREG NORMAN

Lee Trevino

I've always had the knack of shutting things out. That's one of the reasons why I can go around and talk to the crowd and joke and do whatever I want and then five seconds before I execute the shot, I can concentrate on exactly what I want to do. I can shut it all out and then open it back up again.

I think I was trained when I was younger. We never played in a twosome or a threesome, we always played eight guys, ten guys, twelve guys, we played in one large group, so there was always a lot of talking. You were joking and everything, and you'd say, "Wait a minute, let me hit this shot." Then you'd go ahead and hit the shot.

*"A man might be walking around lucky
and not know it unless he tries."*

ARNOLD PALMER

Johnny Miller

I had tremendous focus in the U.S. Open in 1973. Later, I saw pictures of my eyes and face, and I looked like I was possessed. I looked like I was really in the zone. I don't think I started that way, but I got into the zone real quick with my fast start.

I just remember I was very confident with what I was doing, I was not thinking of the consequences, I was just thinking of fairways and knocking it right at the pin. I didn't play safe golf at all, I went right for the pin at every hole, and I was trying to birdie everything I could birdie. I played a lot like a little kid would have played.

My whole thinking was, "I can't wait to hit it, would you hurry up and play so that I can hit it," and "I can't wait to do it because it's going to be fun." I just couldn't wait to hit the shots, they were going to be great.

The zone is the most elusive thing in sports, maybe one of the most exclusive clubs in the world. I think it's a lot like a complex recipe for a dish or a pie and if you miss one ingredient, it doesn't taste quite right. In golf there's a recipe to get into that zone.

I think the zone is really being in harmony with what you're doing. Wanting to do it, wanting to do it for the right reasons, not for money or for greed or for power. That doesn't get you in the zone.

I think love is the secret. I think it's love that gets you in the zone. I really believe it. If you really love to do what you're doing and you want to share your skills with the people watching you and those around you and love the course and just can't wait to play it, and it's going to be fun, then I really believe that you can play some great golf.

If a man really loves what he's doing, he has an infectious appetite for people and they know they're with someone who's got the eye of the tiger, which equates to a feeling of confidence. Then people say, "Geez, I want to do business with that man. He's got it."

My dad always told me, "If you want to be the best, you've got to be willing to do what no one else is willing to do."

Part of the zone is knowing that you're really prepared and you're sacrificing part of yourself and giving some of yourself. It's a feeling of all those ingredients. It's a very complex formula.

*"Enjoy the zone when you're in it,
because it doesn't carry over to the next day."*

SCOTT SIMPSON,
1987 U.S. Open Champion, has logged six PGA tour victories since turning pro in 1977.

"It's not the Zone, it's tempo."

LEE TREVINO

Johnny Miller

Playing in the '73 Open was very interesting. It was at Oakmont, outside of Pittsburgh, considered the hardest course in America since the turn of the century. They prided themselves on how tough they could make it.

I showed up on Tuesday and a lady greeted me by the registration desk and said, "I predict things, and I'm never wrong." She was in her forties, with darkish hair, she didn't seem like any weirdo, but rather a normal person. She merely said, "I predict things, and I'm never wrong. You're going to win the U.S. Open." And I said, "Great. I hope you're right. I'm going to give it my best shot."

I came back on Wednesday and played my practice round. She was there, greeted me at the eighteenth green, and said, "Don't worry, you're going to win."

In those days, you didn't get your pairings until Wednesday, so I went in and got mine, and I was paired with Arnold Palmer which, in Pittsburgh, Pennsylvania, in 1973, was like being thrown into the lion's den.

It's pretty tough. The gallery wasn't too concerned about Johnny Miller. They just wanted their boy Arnie to win. But somehow I played pretty well, 71-69, he had 69-71, we were tied in third place and going along pretty well. The lady came up to me after both rounds and said, "Don't worry, you're going to win." I'm thinking, "This is great."

Saturday I went in and got my mail and there was a letter from Iowa that said, "You're going to win the U.S. Open." No signature, no postmark, nothing. I thought, "Wow, this is really getting strange." So I went out to the first tee and I discovered I had forgotten my yardage card. My yardage card was at the hotel, which was about a thirty-minute drive.

My caddie was a local caddie who didn't know the course very well, and I sort of panicked to say the least. I didn't know if he could help me with the club selection. I hadn't been relying on him at all, so with that feeling of just being run over by a Mack truck, I started. I was five over after seven holes, and shot five over for the day and couldn't wait to find that lady because I'd blown myself right out of the tournament, but she wasn't anywhere to be found.

Sunday morning I went out to the practice tee to hit balls, and the strangest thing happened. When I had about five balls left, a little voice said to me, "Open your stance way up." Just a voice in my mind that said, clear as a bell, "Open your stance way up." I thought, "Why would I want to do that?" And the voice said to me again, "Just open your stance way up."

I tried the last five balls with my stance way open, I mean more open than it had ever been in my life and I really hit them well. I didn't know if it was going to work, but I figured I'd try it anyway. I went to the first hole and knocked it about five feet and made birdie with my open stance. The next hole I hit it stiff with an eight iron for birdie, then I birdied the third, and on the fourth I almost made eagle but settled for another birdie.

I knew I was six strokes back, so it didn't take me too long to figure out that being six back and birdieing the first four, I was probably within two shots of the lead. So I promptly got nervous.

I finished the round pretty strong, shot 63 and ended up winning the U.S. Open by one stroke and breaking the all-time U.S. Open scoring record.

It was pretty exciting. I guess the lady was right, but I never did hear from her ever again. I wish I would have. I'd like to know who she was, but she didn't even tell me her name.

"When I come down the stretch, I have always been able to keep myself together. My attention span gets more acute, my focus is better. I'm able to do what I am supposed to do. I've always been aware of what my abilities are."

JACK NICKLAUS

"The gift of a champion is the ability to compete under pressure, to give a peak performance at a peak moment. Very few are capable of performing in that realm."

STEVE MCFARLAND,
president, U.S. Diving Association

Chris Evert

Trying to articulate the zone is not easy because it's such an indescribable feeling. That moment doesn't happen often, and when it does happen, you feel like you're playing out of your head. Emotionally, mentally, and physically, these three areas are all peaking at the same time. All coming together with 100 percent force.

The feeling is one of almost total relaxation. You aren't feeling any tension or any pressure and physically your strokes are just flowing, every ball you hit is going in. Emotionally you're really calm. There's no strain involved. It's a euphoric feeling. The feeling that whatever you touch turns to gold. Whatever you do, whatever decision you make on the court, whatever stroke or shot you try, you know it's going to work.

You can't miss anything. It's like you anticipate, way ahead of time, earlier than usual, where the ball is going and you also know where you're going to hit the ball before you hit it.

Sometimes you hit the ball, and it's like you decide at the last minute where to hit it, but it's that knowledge, that confidence, and also that freedom of just letting go, letting the strokes flow. Everything seems slower so you have more time to adjust.

You feel one with the fans. You don't feel like you're on the court and the fans are cheering, you don't feel like they're separate from you. You just feel at one and at peace with the whole scene.

You're aware of them in a sense because you're aware of

their appreciation and you're aware that they're helping you to reach this extreme, but on the other hand, you're not distracted to the point where you're hearing the clapping and the cheering or a baby crying. You're not really hearing the distractive part of the crowd, but you're hearing the positive part of it, the appreciation that they have for you.

It's a great feeling. I think that was part of the reason why my career was so long. I think some players go through life without feeling this, and I think this is the thing that keeps players going.

*"You're always striving to play
that perfect match."*

CHRIS EVERT

*"What I got from tennis was a search for
excellence, improvement, to be as good as I
could be as a tennis player. I love to compete
and I want to win, but mostly I want to run and
have fun and see how good I can be."*

MARTINA NAVRATILOVA
has won more tennis matches than any other player in history,
167 singles titles and 56 Grand Slam Championships

Bart Conner

You wish you could bottle it up and save it for another day. I don't know anyone who's been able to find it and re-create it at will. It has a lot to do with circumstances. Everything falling in place. The zone, to me, is the ultimate rush.

In gymnastics you're flying and you're flipping and twisting. There's a little danger to it and yet you feel just absolutely fearless. You might be doing a triple back off the high bar, but you're so *on* that it's like things slow down and you just see the picture so beautifully, so vividly.

You might be doing three flips through the air and although you can't visually spot the ground every time you flip past it, you still know exactly where it is. You know exactly where you are. You know you're making the right decisions. Things are just falling into place. You're never surprised.

"When it happens
you are in total control.
Nothing bothers you."

TOM KITE

Bill Walton

Everything slows down. It's like everybody is wearing cement shoes, the ball is in slow motion, everything slows down except you, and you feel like you're operating at a different speed and at a different level than anybody else.

The clarity of your vision, the clarity of your senses is maxed out, and everybody else looks like their eyes are just fogged over.

You try to call it up, but you really can't. So what you try to do is re-create the same situation each and every game by routine, by the timing of your pregame meal, the routine of your getting dressed, the routine of your thoughts, the routine of your nap, the routine of the whole day. But what really brings it on is the intensity of the actual game and the respect of knowing that the opposition can beat you.

If you know deep in your heart that the other guy can't beat you at all, has no chance of beating you, then it's hard to get to that level. But if you're playing against the Jabbars or the Dr. J's or the Larry Birds or Magic, then you know, "Hey, they've got a chance to beat me." Then your chances of being red-hot or being the superstar in that game are so much greater.

You don't see the crowd. Really all you can see is to the boundary of the court. You can't see the players on the bench. You can see the coach but not the guys on the bench. You don't see the crowd, but you know they're there. It's just a big fog, and it's like having a wall around the court, and that's the only thing you can deal with.

It's just a big mass of something that is great.

*"Use the crowd to feed your body
the great pain-killers that allow you
to push beyond the normal levels of pain."*

BILL WALTON

*"You become addicted
to the adrenalin of the game."*

BOB TRUMPY

*"One of the things that always amazed me
was that a linebacker could hit me, really
nail me, knock me down, and I'd get up,
turn around, and I could immediately
find the quarterback."*

BOB TRUMPY

Bob Trumpy

It was like being in a tunnel and being blinded by a bright light. When I came out of the other end of the tunnel, I was in the end zone and my teammates were celebrating. To this day I still don't remember what I did.

There would be times when there was total darkness in the tunnel. I simply don't remember plays that happened. Sometimes they were good, sometimes they were bad. I don't remember them.

The people in the stands. I didn't notice them. I'd walk by people that I knew and I didn't recognize them on game day. I was always in this tunnel. It wasn't a small tunnel. It was a big tunnel. It incorporated the sidelines. It didn't really go to the stands. It was like a giant Quonset hut over the football field.

When the defense was playing, I'd go to the sideline, and I was out of the tunnel. When I was out of it, I'd notice the fans. But when I was on the field, it was like a transparent curtain that was just there. I don't know how to describe it other than it went from sideline to sideline. It was high enough so that no matter how high the ball was thrown, it would stay in the tunnel.

I don't have very good eyesight but there were several instances where I swear this happened. I'd get a contact lens knocked out of my eye and my vision was still perfect in that eye. I'd go to the sideline, things would get fuzzy, and that's when I'd realize that my contact lens was gone.

*"The tunnel was something I really enjoyed.
It was a safe place."*

BOB TRUMPY

*"The first time it didn't happen
was my first All-Star Game.
It scared me to death.
The tunnel wasn't there.
Finally I realized because the game was
unimportant, winning didn't have any meaning."*

BOB TRUMPY

*"I've found nothing
that comes close to the tunnel
outside of athletics.
Zero.
It's very frustrating."*

BOB TRUMPY

Ahmad Rashad

During the course of a sixty-minute game there were times when our opponent's intensity or attention span would dip. That would be the difference. If you could take advantage of that little dip, and it only happened a couple, maybe three times a game, then you could win. You had to take advantage of it when it happened and to do that you had to be focused.

In the NFL the athletic ability is pretty much the same. I think what separates the winners from the losers is the ability to focus. It's the ability after a practice or after a game to sit and look back and start to think, "What was the difference in being able to make a catch and not make a catch?" You try to think back to what mentally went through your mind and find that mindset, find where you were at that particular moment and then put yourself into that space every single Sunday.

Once you're able to find it, to get yourself mentally in that space, once you're able to put yourself in there every single week your confidence level is so high that you're unstoppable at that point. You're just unstoppable.

The superstars do it more times than not. I think there's a level of difference between players. I think all pros do it every now and then. Stars do it more often than every now and then, and superstars do it every single time they play.

It's clarity. You've got to visualize yourself making great plays. If you've never made a great play, it's hard to visualize. Coaches go to average players and say, "Visualize yourself doing great things." That's hard to do.

I always said that my greatest attribute as a pro was that I was steady. Every week you knew I was going to do something. And I never dipped. I never had a totally bad game. That consistency was something that I felt very proud of. Every week you were going to get something out of me. That's what the coach expected from me, that's what I expected from myself.

I also felt as an entertainer that I was going to give the people that too. If you came out to watch me play, you're going to watch me do something great.

It was an arena for me to perform in. I just enjoyed every single bit of it. I loved the pressure. I wanted to be the guy if it were third and eighteen to get the first down. "Throw it over here. I'll make the catch." Or if it was the last play of the game I thought, "Throw it to me. I'll make that catch."

I remember the coaches calling that Hail Mary against Cleveland. As I trotted out to my position I made up my mind that I wasn't going to run down there and jump up. I was going to wait for a rebound.

Because everyone I'd ever watched jumped up and nobody ever caught it out of that crowd. But I'd always see it knocked away, and the ball would float over to a player who was just standing there waiting for it.

So I trailed everybody down. I never tried to get up in there, in the group. I figured, "If this baby's tipped, I got about an 80 percent chance of catching it because I can go left, I can go right, I can even back up. But if I get in that crowd, I've got one shot. Jump and catch it." And nobody ever does that. I was very calm, I wasn't hyped up, like "Oh, I've got to catch it."

It was like "Uh huh, okay, now." And as I was running down, I was watching everybody. "Okay, Sammy's going over there, here comes Tom, all right, they'll all jump and . . .

whoop . . . they . . . whoop . . . it's right here." I caught it one-handed. It wasn't like I dove and fought . . . I just reached out and caught it one-handed, put it on my hip and backed into the end zone. It wasn't a big deal.

AHMAD RASHAD, former All-Pro wide receiver with the Minnesota Vikings (1976 to 1982) and current NBC Sports broadcaster

---

"Some players with a lot of athletic ability
just go out and play.
Then after four or five years
you don't hear about them anymore.
The smart guys figure it out,
and they play ten, twelve years.
They do it mentally more than they
do it physically."

AHMAD RASHAD

"Never let out all your hose until you know
where the fire is."

JOHN MADDEN,
Super Bowl XI – winning coach with the Oakland Raiders, now NFL television analyst with the Fox network

Jimmy Cefalo

I can remember wondering whether or not I wanted to catch that pass in Super Bowl XVII while it was coming down. I was battling myself mentally. I don't know if all ballplayers do that. Maybe just the ones who are cerebral.

It was over my head. It was a very bad throw from David Woodley. It was one of those balls thrown directly over my head and the ball was actually going out-of-bounds. I was going to get waylaid. I knew I was. I knew it was going to hurt, and I had no control over the circumstances.

A receiver can take one little step here or one little step there and get out of a real deadly situation. I was debating whether or not I wanted to pay the price of trying to catch this ball.

The ball was very clear as it came through the air. It seemed like it was going to stay up there for sixty seconds. It was like, "Do I really want to do this? I know that safety is going to really hit me, and yeah, this is the Super Bowl but I'm not a masochist. Oh, all right, here it is." And I caught it. And I scored. What a strange thing though. It changed my whole life, catching that ball.

People always remember that I had a long touchdown reception in the Super Bowl, it's something that I'm very proud of, it's the one play people remember. It changed my career. But when it was in the air, I was still debating whether or not I wanted to catch that ball.

"The hardest catch
is when you're wide open
in the end zone.
You're trying to position yourself
for the photographers.
You want a big smile,
because you know,
if you catch it,
you're going to be on the front page
of tomorrow's newspaper."

JIMMY CEFALO

"It's all right to be Goliath,
but always act like David."

PHIL KNIGHT,
founder, president, and CEO of Nike

Johnny Bench

Some days I just knew I was going to get a pitch that I could hit, and if they gave me a pitch to hit, I was going to hit a home run, no matter who or what. I told Tom Seaver one night that on the first pitch he threw me, I was going to hit a home run, and I did.

Gary Carter was catching one day in Montreal and a lefthander was pitching. He threw me a fastball away and missed. Gary put the sign down, the guy went into the stretch, and I said, "Watch this one, kid," and hit it out of the park.

I hit it when Chuck Connors was sitting in the stands one night. He had played in a golf tournament in Cincinnati and he'd said, "I'm going to birdie this hole for Johnny Bench," and he did.

That night Ray Sadecki was pitching. Chuck was sitting in the front row, down by the on-deck circle, and I said, "Watch this one." He said, "Home run." And I said, "Yeah." First pitch, I hit it out of the ballpark.

"Every great batter
works on the theory
that the pitcher is more afraid of him
than he is of the pitcher."

TY COBB
is arguably baseball's greatest player of all time; the leader in career batting average (.367) and runs scored (2,245).

---

*"As far as Jack Nicklaus is concerned, pressure
has something to do with the air in your tires.
It is not something that affects him
on the golf course."*

THOMAS BONK,
staff writer for the *Los Angeles Times*

*"My theory is that people
who are so supremely talented
and who do things so very well
aren't necessarily articulate
or as aware of what they do.
It's those of us who only had a peek behind the
curtain that spend our lives trying to figure it out,
trying to decipher it."*

STEVE MCFARLAND

Charlie Jones

I'll always remember my first Major League Baseball telecast. It was in 1966 and I was announcing the Dallas-Fort Worth Spurs in the Texas League when I got the call from NBC Sports to go to Pittsburgh for the backup Game of the Week on Saturday with Tony Kubek. This was Tony's rookie year with the network.

I flew into Pittsburgh on Friday and immediately went to Forbes Field as my knowledge of the National League was rather skimpy at that time.

That night I had the good fortune to meet Bob Prince, the Hall of Fame broadcaster for the Pittsburgh Pirates. When Bob found out this was my Major League Baseball debut he said, in that great gravelly voice, "Kid, come with me." He immediately took me under his wing and included me in everything he did that night.

Bob invited me to sit in his radio booth, and his broadcast was a complete outline for me to follow the next day. He gave a minibio on every player including all the statistics, not only for the Pirates but also for the Cincinnati Reds, and he mixed in anecdotes I could use.

I was sitting right behind him just taking note after note after note. Then after the game Bob drove me downtown to his club where we had a late night snack, a couple of drinks, and went over Saturday's starting pitchers.

I'll always remember that night because Bob Prince really went out of his way to help me prepare for my first Major League Baseball broadcast.

The next morning dawned bright and sunny in

Pittsburgh. However, it was raining at the site of the primary game. By eleven o'clock that game had been called which meant our game had the full network. I was really excited when Roy Hammerman, our producer, dropped this little bomb on us, but Tony just said, "I'll be back in a moment," and he promptly disappeared.

Now it was fifteen minutes before the game and no Tony. Now it was ten minutes before the game and still no Tony. Finally, five minutes before air, a pale-faced Tony Kubek slid into the broadcast booth. I asked, "Where've you been?" Kubek said, "I've been throwing up. I'm not ready to go national." But of course he was. Tony did an excellent job and went on to become one of the great baseball TV analysts of all time.

Author's note: A few years later Bob Prince and I worked together on, of all things, the NBC telecast of the East-West Shrine Football Game.

"Never look where you're going. Always look where you want to go."

BOB ERNST,
rowing coach at the University of Washington

Don Baylor

In '79, my MVP year with the California Angels, I had total concentration. I reminded myself of turning a water faucet on and off, hot and cold. Every time I was in a crucial situation that water always had to be hot, because I was the one right in the middle of everything.

The ball seemed to stop in motion because I'd concentrated so much. I'd played the game before it was played. I spent an hour in a room, just by myself, getting my mind totally ready to play. I would talk myself into watching the pitcher's motion by closing my eyes in that dark room, and once I came out, I was almost in a hypnotic state.

On days when it was there, the ball just came up to the plate and stopped for me. I said, "Okay, I'm going to hit this ball into left center," or "I'm going to hit it to right center." Being in the zone, that's what happens. Everything just stops. You're not hurried in anything you do. It just happens.

*"Concentration is
the ability to think about absolutely nothing
when it is absolutely necessary."*

RAY KNIGHT,
manager, Cincinnati Reds

When I'm in the zone, I'm totally engulfed in just that moment. Nothing distracts me at all. It would be just that pitch, that particular pitch, and there's only that one pitch. That's the only thing there is in the whole world.

I'm in sync with my catcher. I don't even shake the catcher off. I just keep staring in until I see the right sign. In shaking my head, I feel like that's a negative response and I don't want anything negative, so I just stare or maybe I'll just barely shake my head.

You might not be able to pick it up, but my catcher can. If I'm really into the zone, I don't like to shake my head at all. I just keep staring at his glove and his fingers, seeing the right fingers and then go ahead and execute the pitch, so that nothing breaks my tunnel vision. It's a tunnel vision that travels right into the catcher's glove.

There is no strike zone. There is no hitter up there. I'm throwing to the glove. It doesn't matter if there's a hitter up there or not, I'm going to throw the same pitch.

The hitter doesn't exist, because he's only there after the ball's left my hand and then he becomes part of the game. He's not part of the game when he's standing there, because he has nothing to do with the way I'm going to throw the ball, other than strategy. But after that has been determined, the only thing that's left is execution, so the batter doesn't even exist.

Once I get on that little circle of dirt, that's my key that now I'm thinking about pitching. I allow my thoughts to wander and to think about the game and strategy when I'm out on the grass but when I'm on the dirt, then I'm thinking about pitching. Even one step beyond that, when my spikes touch the rubber I'm thinking about execution.

With a key pitch, when I have a lot of energy, my body has a tendency to do things in a bigger way and that can create problems. I overthrow my curve ball. I hang it or I try and throw it too hard and it won't break. Or I pull it into the ground because I have so much adrenaline and strength.

I think back to other times when I had adrenaline and I think of keys to help me execute. For a sinking fastball, I might think, "I want to keep the ball to the inside part of my hand this time and make sure there's some pressure on my index finger because that'll make sure the ball will sink."

You're a different person every time you walk out to the mound. For me, about one out of every five outings, I walk out there and it just flows out of my body, and I really don't even need to think about concentrating, I don't think about mechanics. My natural athletic ability just happens to click. But the other four out of five times, I'm making adjustments every single pitch, every single inning. I'm working at it. It might not look like it but I'm working at it. And what I'm working at is trying to find a rhythm, trying to find the correct mechanical adjustment, trying to find the thing that makes me click as far as concentration.

Also, I have to fight my game face. If it comes on too early, it expends a lot of energy and I get tired early in the game. I'll fight it, if I see it's coming on the night before a game. I'll do things like watch a movie that I can really get involved in or start playing intensely with the kids or get into a deep conversation with my wife.

When I'm in the car going to the ballpark, that's a great time to put my game face on. That's a real good time to start thinking about the game. Then I get to the ballpark, I park the car and I'm starting to get into a zone. I go in and get my uniform on, I go into batting practice and do all the things I need to do to get ready.

When we won the World Series in '88, I don't remember throwing those final pitches. I don't remember any of the celebrating, except for saying, "I'm going to Disneyland," because I've seen that on TV. It wasn't until I got almost completely off the field in front of our dugout at Oakland and looked up in the stands for my wife Jamie. I finally saw her, and that's when I felt that my game face left.

Then I smiled, I waved to her and I cheered. All of a sudden a great rush of emotion came over me and I was happy that we'd won. I wasn't happy that we won for about four or five minutes. Even though I was cheering and smiling in the footage, I can remember internally I wasn't happy yet. My game face was still there. It wouldn't allow me to relax and it wouldn't allow me to say, "Hey, this is over. You can be happy now." It wasn't until I saw Jamie and she was hugging my dad and crying that it finally released and kicked in.

The feeling was amazing. But it doesn't last very long. That's the thing about the way God created humans. Pleasure doesn't last very long. The first question they ask you is, "Can you repeat?" They don't let you enjoy it for five minutes.

OREL HERSHISER, who pitched first for the Dodgers, then for the Indians, is the all-time leader in most consecutive scoreless innings (59 in 1988). He was the 1988 Cy Young Award winner and World Series MVP.

*"The great different between men is sacrifice, in
self-denial and fearlessness and humility,
in love and loyalty and the perfectly disciplined
will. This is not only the difference between
men, but this is the difference between
great men and little men."*

VINCE LOMBARDI,
head coach who led his Green Bay Packers to victory
in Super Bowls I and II

*"Great athletes have an inner strength,
something you cannot define."*

GARY PLAYER

*"Do not let the desire to win sacrifice a
commitment to sportsmanship and fair play."*

STEPHANIE DEIBLER,
senior softball player for Allentown College of
St. Francis de Sales, Center Valley, Pennsylvania

I have been in the zone many times when I have been driving in the national championships, but it only happened once outside of drag racing. It was a near accident on a bridge. I was towing my truck and trailer and I came up over the rise where the boats go through the draw, over on the Howard Franklin Bridge in Tampa.

Just as I came over the draw, there was a stalled car about five hundred yards away in my lane. Now this is a bridge with two lanes going in the same direction. I was in the right-hand lane and beside me there was traffic, so I couldn't move into the left-hand lane. The stalled car was a little Pinto and the guy was standing in back of it, waving his arms.

I stepped down on the brake and my truck wouldn't stop. The trailer brakes had become damaged. I had no trailer brakes.

My mind quickly underwent this strange phenomenon. I thought the brakes weren't hooked up, I thought somebody had not plugged in the receptacle; later I found out it was a damaged wire . . . and I thought "I'm fixin' to kill this guy and it's not totally my fault, but if I had been prepared properly it wouldn't have happened."

First I went into a skid and started to go through the railing. I brought it out of that. Everything was real slow for about, I'd say, five or six seconds.

I swerved the vehicle, the truck and trailer went sideways, it started to jackknife around and the car on the left side of me dropped off just enough to give me a tiny hole. I worked the truck and trailer into that hole and brought it out of the skid all in the same motion. I missed him. It was a miracle.

It was a strange thing. Everything got real slow and quiet. That's the only time it's ever happened outside of racing. It was activated at that moment when I thought how terrible it was that I was fixin' to kill another human being and it really didn't have to happen. This guy was dead. There was no way he could have survived. He would have been torn to pieces when my truck hit his Pinto.

He was paralyzed when he realized what was happening. He just stood there. He could have jumped out of the way but he didn't. Just stood there like a frog waiting for the snake.

The truck was skidding. That great big trailer just pushed it like it was nothing. The trailer weighed 22,000 pounds and the truck weighed 6,000. I'd been running about fifty-five miles per hour, so you know there wasn't a prayer.

My wife was there and it scared her half to death. My crew chief was sitting behind me and said he'd never seen anything like it in his entire life. There are some strange things that happen to your mind.

We got off the bridge at the other end, pulled over to the side, and all got down on the ground and held hands and prayed. Thanked God.

"BIG DADDY" DON GARLITS is a drag race champion and has won thirty-five NHRA top fuel events. He is credited with developing the rear-engine dragster.

John Naber

In the Montreal Olympics I felt like I was moving through a sea of molasses. Everything moved in slow motion. Sounds seemed as if they were coming from the end of a distant tunnel. Everything on the periphery of my view was fuzzy.

It was as if you were looking at the fine engraving on a postage stamp with a magnifying glass and the edge of the stamp would basically just disappear from your view. You would be so totally concentrated on the middle of the stamp that nothing else really mattered and certainly the table that the stamp was on or the room that the table was in would be irrelevant.

That's the way it was. I put one foot in front of the other, just walking. My only concentration was that thin little walk on the way to the starting blocks. I heard every sound in the world as if from a distance, but I was waiting to hear the sound of the starter say, "Take your marks," and that sound I heard clearly.

I had programmed myself as to what to listen for. It's like when you're in an airport reading a newspaper, you hear public address pages going on all the time and you never pay any attention to them. But the moment the words "John Naber, would you please go to a white courtesy phone" are said, your ears pick it right up.

The same way you're tuned to hearing your own name is the way you're tuned to hearing only important feedback. That's why a lover, a spouse, or a coach will look you in the face and say, "Good luck," and you don't even see them because they're not germane, they're not important right now.

Once the gun sounds that same feeling continues until that small focus of concentration slowly grows larger and larger, so that when you're at the end of the race, wham, it hits you like a ton of bricks; there's this whole arena filled with 17,000 people cheering their heads off. Suddenly it's as if someone turns the volume up.

The moment the race is over you join real time and that's when it just overwhelms you. It's like a magical experience.

"It's not only how you compete,
but also how you control
the competitive circumstances."

FRANK SHORTER

"I'm always proud of anyone who takes a good
challenge and wins."

JACK NICKLAUS

Frank Shorter

You can become so focused on the effort that you aren't aware of the extraneous stuff. I've seen videos of the Montreal Olympic Marathon in '76, and it rained like hell during the race.

I don't remember any rain. I remember it being wet, but I don't remember the rain. I remember the streets being wet, but I don't remember it raining. My mind was just focusing on trying to get there first.

I wanted to get to that point about halfway, when I was going to make my move. I wanted to stay as relaxed as I could until I got to that point and then break away when I got there.

That's exactly what I did except that Waldemar Cierpinski of East Germany stayed with me. The first time in Munich in 1972, nobody went with me and I won the gold medal. I did it the same way in Montreal, but this time they knew it was coming.

It's like they know you're going to do it, but you do it anyway because they really can't keep up with you. It's that kind of mindset. But this time Cierpinski was ready. He won the gold and I got the silver.

"In 1972, as soon as my feet hit the floor in the morning, I couldn't wait to start the Marathon. In '76, my feet hit the floor, and I wanted to go back to bed."

Frank Shorter

*"No athlete enters a race
sure that he's going to win."*

SIR ROGER BANNISTER
in 1954 became the first person to break the four-minute
mile barrier.

*"Whether you're in a marathon race
or you're trying to outdo someone in the clothing
business, you're better off if your competition
is constantly watching you
and paying more attention to you
than they are to their race or their business."*

FRANK SHORTER

*"Fourth place in the Olympics is the worst place
you can ever finish."*

STEVE PREFONTAINE
is the only track star ever to hold the U.S. records in every
distance from 2,000 to 10,000 meters. He finished fourth in
the 5,000 meters in the 1972 Olympics.

Bruce Jenner

I determine my future. I don't let anything on the outside of me determine my future. I'm in control. The crowd doesn't have anything to do with it, other competitors don't have anything to do with it, the jet that's flying over doesn't have anything to do with it. If I'm going to do well, it's going to come from inside me. That's what's going to determine it. So you just focus. Everything just goes "zip," right inside.

You make what you're doing extremely important in your life. It comes with commitment. Making a commitment to yourself and saying this is important in my life. It is important I do well. This is my life.

When you make those commitments to yourself, then you become extremely focused and extremely determined. It's a funny thing. You don't go around telling people, your competitors or the media. But down deep inside, inwardly, the fire burns.

I made a commitment years in advance but the final one came about twelve months before the Montreal Games. I made that final commitment to myself that I was not going to be satisfied with second, that I would not be satisfied with any position but winning.

*"Participating in athletic competition
is an analogy for real life. You have to
prepare for it. Then you go through the event.
Then there's the post-event. It's like life. That's
why sports are so special."*

DR. THOMAS TUTKO
professor of sports psychology at San Jose State University

*"I want to be remembered as a person who
felt there was no limitation to what the
human body and mind can do and be the
inspiration to lead people to do things
they never hoped to do."*

CARL LEWIS

Tim Daggett

Let me refresh you a little bit. We (U.S.A.) had gone through the entire compulsories and the first five events of the optionals in the finals of the Los Angeles Olympics.

We're on high bar and the Chinese are on floor, our last events. They're the reigning world champions, so they're the favorites to win. We were certainly not supposed to win.

The last event for us was high bar. Now this is going to sound a little corny to you. My best friend Peter Vidmar was also on that team. We had trained real hard together getting ready for the '84 Games. In gymnastics there are six events, and you usually do all six events in a workout.

There's an Olympic rotation. In our workouts we always followed the Olympic rotation floor exercise, pommel horse, still rings, vault, parallel bars, and high bar. We would follow that every single day. The reason was that we were hoping for that rotation in the Olympic Games, because if that was the case then we would be leading the competition after the compulsories. So first of all, it was optimistic thinking.

After the compulsories they rank the teams, and the first place team gets the standard Olympic rotation which starts on floor and finishes on high bar. The second place team starts on pommel horse, the third on still rings, and so on down the line.

So being optimistic during our four years of preparation at UCLA, we would start every workout every day on floor exercise and progress all the way through. We were very, very motivated people. Peter and I would come into the gym and give 100 percent on floor exercise. It would go great because we were fresh from a night's rest.

Then we would go on to pommel horse. We both medaled on that event in the Olympics, so it was a good event for us. We got through the horse, no problem at all. Then we moved to rings, and we're starting to get a little tired now, but we're still pretty fresh, and finally we would get to the last event, high bar.

We started practice at two in the afternoon and it's now sometime after seven o'clock in the evening. The gym is desolate, deserted, everybody else is already studying or at the dormitory eating, and all of a sudden we're not as psyched as we were five hours before.

Obviously, just because the event comes at the end of the workout or the end of the competition, as opposed to the beginning, it's just as important. You still have to try just as hard.

This is a true story but it does sound a little far-fetched. First of all, high bar is a very dangerous event. When you're letting go of the bar and flying fifteen feet in the air, you better have all your wits about you and you better be motivated to catch the bar or be ready for a big fall. So we'd play this little game.

We'd imagined it was the Olympic Games every single practice for the last six or seven months. When we'd get to the high bar, I'd announce to an empty Pauley Pavilion, "Next up for the United States of America, Peter Vidmar on the high bar, the Chinese on floor, the Soviets on pommel horse. Tim Daggett is sixth and both gymnasts need a perfect ten for the United States to win the Gold Medal."

We put ourselves in that exact position. I can remember going up, in practice, saluting my coach, Makoto Sakamoto, knowing that I was in the Olympic venue, knowing that I was last up for the Americans, knowing that if I did the best routine of my life, if I did a perfect ten, if I stuck my dismount, that we would win the gold.

I can remember taking a little step on a dismount in practice and being devastated until the next day when I had the chance to do it all over again and prepare just a little bit more. Or if I did a perfect routine and stuck my dismount I felt that day, that evening, like I had won the Olympic Games. It was my food, my motivation, my energy to keep going.

I say all this because right at that moment when it's all in your grasp, it's overwhelming—July 31, 1984—the amazing thing was that Peter and I were in that exact situation. I was fifth up for the Americans, Peter was sixth, the Chinese were on floor. We were neck and neck with them although we weren't supposed to be.

Now suddenly we had to deal with it. It was a little scary but I just told myself that I had done this all before. I remember walking over to Peter who is pacing back and forth, and I'm pacing back and forth, and something just clicked right at that second and I said, "Peter, we've done it before, we've done it a thousand times, we can do it again." He said the same thing back to me, and I just knew I was going to do it.

I did the best routine of my life and scored a perfect ten. At that point Peter didn't even have to perform because we had already won the gold, as our first five scores were high enough to beat the Chinese.

As soon as I landed, it was like BOOM! I knew as soon as I stuck my dismount. I don't know why, but I just knew I was going to get a ten, I knew it, I knew that a 10 would win it right there, I knew that I had done it for the U.S.

It was very much like what people talk about who've had

a near-death experience, where their life flashes before their eyes. I can remember my brain just went crazy. I remembered walking into the gym the first time when I was nine years old, seeing that guy on the high bar, seeing him let go of the bar and fly through the air, and how I wanted to be like him. I remembered my first state championships, I remembered when I hurt myself for the first time, I remembered all the people telling me I was never going to make it. I remembered qualifying for my first national team, I remembered making my first world team, I remembered qualifying for the Olympic Games.

All of these things just went bang, bang, bang, bang, bang, bang, bang in my head. Boy, it was wonderful.

Tim Daggett

This actually happened the next day, the day after our performance that clinched the Gold Medal in the '84 Olympics.

I was walking around Westwood Village. First of all, something was happening to me that had never happened before. People were pointing. "There's that guy. There's that guy. He was one of the gymnasts, right?"

Then this young Mexican woman came up to me and said, "Oh my, you're one of those boys that won the gold medal last night. You know, I've been living in this country for many, many years now, and I think it's a beautiful country, but just recently I got my American citizenship. I didn't really know if this was right for me. All of my relatives, all of my friends, they're still in Mexico. I didn't think I was a true American. But last night when you won, and when you had that gold medal wrapped around your neck, I cried for the first time and I felt proud to be an American."

TIM DAGGETT, Olympic gold-medal winner in gymnastics in the 1984 games

Michele Mitchell-Rocha

It was a feeling I had when I woke up, and it had nothing to do with what I ate or where I was sleeping or if I had a lot of rest or not. It was like a little smile when I woke up. When that smile was there, I knew it was going to be a good day. I knew I was going to win because there was a little voice inside that smile and it told me so.

I feel like it's all predestined. I've read the book but I just have to keep flipping the pages. I know what the ending's going to be but I'm not quite sure what's going to be on each page, so I just keep flipping them.

That's why, if I had that feeling and there was some catastrophe along the way, it became, "Well, this is a test but I still know what the end result is going to be. This just makes it more exciting."

In '84 when I was at the Los Angeles Olympic Games, the first day I walked into the pool—that was my first major international competition. I'd never even seen the Chinese, much less knew how to compete against them. I looked way down to the other end of the pool, opposite the dive wall where they have the award platform, and my eyes just kept falling to the second-place victory stand.

Someone could say, "Oh, yeah, that was just a self-fulfilling prophecy," but it was too strong a feeling. So even then, the day I walked into the Olympic Games, I knew where I was going to finish before I ever started.

The morning of the finals I woke up with that little smile and the feeling that I was going to do well. But again, when I got to the pool I kept looking at the second-place victory stand. I knew I was going to get second, no matter what. To me in '84 that was the greatest thing on earth, when I got second place and won the silver medal.

"Fear is a huge factor in diving.
It's a part of the sport,
it's a part of overcoming the sport,
it's a part of the thrill of the sport."

MICHELE MITCHELL-ROCHA

"When I was up on the tower,
thirty-three feet above the water,
my blood pressure was lower then than it was
when I was sitting on the couch at home.
As soon as the competition pressure would go up,
I would just calm down."

MICHELE MITCHELL-ROCHA

Michele Mitchell-Rocha

The 1988 Olympics in Seoul was the only time that I second-guessed myself, after my little voice told me what was going to happen.

I had awakened that morning knowing I was going to win the gold medal, I was just absolutely sure of it. Charlie Jones was broadcasting for NBC, and I didn't even tell him because I didn't want to jinx myself, but I knew I was going to win.

Going into the last dive it was close enough so that all I had to do was a good dive, nothing fantastic, just a good dive and I was going to beat the Chinese girl and win the gold medal and be the first gold medalist for the United States in these Olympic Games.

I was standing on the seven-meter tower preparing for my dive. It was my hip-pocket dive, the one I could just pull out of my back pocket, and know it was going to be there. Instead of just relaxing and thinking about my dive I made the mistake of thinking what it would all mean six months from now. What it was going to be like to be the first gold medalist, all the excitement and all the thrills, and I started going beyond the moment of the dive. I'd never done that before in competition, actually gone beyond the moment and I thought, "Gee, if I win the Gold Medal I'm going to have all these interviews, I'm going to do all these commercials, and I'm going to make all this money."

I climbed up to the ten-meter platform, and I was totally relaxed and focused, but I knew I had to make a decision. The tower was slippery and if I got right out on the edge I took a big risk of slipping and possibly failing the dive and not getting the gold medal. But if I stayed back and shortened up my run so if I did slide I wouldn't slide off the end of the tower, then I could do my front three-and-a-half, I could still get it in. I knew that dive, I knew where it was better than anyone.

I decided to stay back, and that was the first time ever in competition that I didn't go for it. That, in combination with thinking ahead of the moment, made me do the dive less than perfectly, and I ended up getting second place by three points.

I knew when I hit the water that I'd made the wrong decision by being conservative instead of going for it. It was my little voice telling me, "See, you should have gone with what you knew worked. Now I've got to punish you for going beyond the moment."

"On one hand,
you don't want to be greedy and say,
'Yeah, I'm disappointed with the silver,'
but then on the other hand, the
reality is I should have won the gold."

MICHELE MITCHELL-ROCHA

Michele Mitchell-Rocha

The highlight of my career was in '85. We were in China and the pool in Shanghai was filled with 20,000 people because diving is such a popular sport in Asia.

The girl who had defeated me in the Olympics in '84, Zhu Ji Hong, was just ahead of me in the standings and she really drilled her final dive. The big scoreboard flashed her points, eight-and-a halves and nines, and the crowd went berserk because they thought, "Oh, she beat that American girl again. The Chinese can't be defeated." The crowd was going nuts.

I was up next. I was doing my hardest dive, an inward three-and-a half. I was the only woman in the world doing that dive at that time, and I needed nines on it to win. The scoreboard projected that fact: "Needs 85 points to win" which is almost impossible.

As I walked to the end of the platform, the crowd, instead of being quiet and polite like most crowds, started tinkling their tea cups, real china tea cups. Twenty-thousand Chinese were tinkling their tea cups on their seats and on the cement floor, and they were clapping randomly to fluster me.

With that dive my back was to the arena. I couldn't see what they were doing, so it didn't dawn on me what was happening. All I heard was this odd noise. Then as I started raising my arms for the dive, I realized they were trying to distract me.

This was that threat "don't get me mad because of what I might do." Well, I got really mad. In about two seconds I thought, "This is bullshit. Here I am in the middle of China, trying to do my dive, and 20,000 people are trying to distract me so this Chinese girl can beat me again. It's just not going to happen." I got really really mad and said a few magical words to myself and took off.

I remember very clearly it was a slow-motion dive. I remember everything about that dive. I remember I had the perfect takeoff. It was like I was watching myself through a video camera sitting in the stands, like I had changed perspective and was watching myself from an out-of-body point-of-view.

I saw my dive go in the water straight up and down. As soon as I hit the water physically, I knew that I had won. I just knew it. When I came up, you'd expect that performing a dive that well the crowd would be cheering wildly, but the whole place, 20,000 people, were silent. The only ones who were cheering were the six other members of the American team. Twenty-thousand Chinese had been silenced because they had challenged me to beat their diver, and they were trying to do it in an unfair way. I basically said, "In your face."

When the scores came up, I got nine nine-and-a-halves and defeated Zhu Ji Hong. And I had done it in China. I was the first woman to win in China, and it was the first gold medal of the World Championships. Talk about a great feeling. Listening to our National Anthem in what was then Communist China was a big thrill.

That was one of the few times when my mental video camera, instead of playing from an internal point of view, actually changed to an external. It was as if I was sitting in the audience, watching myself dive. That was a neat experience.

Mom and Dad usually used those trips as an excuse. You know, spend $10,000 to watch your daughter dive. But they didn't go to China, so that night I called them collect. It was about three in the morning Arizona time, and who else but your parents would accept a collect call from Shanghai.

My dad answered, and I said, "Dad?" and he said, "Yeah, yeah, how are you doing? Did you compete?" and I said, "Dad, you're talking to the World Champion." There was silence on the other end of the phone, and then I could hear the tears dropping on his face.

MICHELE MITCHELL-ROCHA, Olympic platform diver, won the silver medal in the Los Angeles and Seoul games, and the World Championship in Shanghai. She is now the diving coach at the University of Arizona.

EPILOGUE

While Bart Conner and Tim Daggett were capturing their 1984 Gymnastic gold medals at Pauley Pavilion on the campus of UCLA, across town at the McDonald's Pool on the campus of the University of Southern California the saga of nineteen-year old Pablo Morales began.

In the finals of the 100-meter butterfly, Pablo was just touched out by Michael Gross of West Germany for the gold. He won the silver, but it was just the beginning. Two years later Pablo set the world record in the 100 fly, and in 1988 he was the favorite going into the Olympic Trials in Indianapolis for the Games in Seoul.

But Pablo had an absolutely horrible week in Indianapolis, finishing third and failing to make the team (only the first and second place finishers in each swimming event go to the Olympics). He then retired, returned to Stanford where he completed his senior year, and after graduating went to Columbia University Law School in New York City.

During his second year there, a family tragedy occurred: his mother, Blanca, became seriously ill and then died from cancer. It was a difficult time for Pablo, but it was at this difficult time that he came to grips with his Olympic ambition. He still had some unfinished business. He would swim again.

So Pablo Morales took a leave of absence from his senior year at Columbia Law School, traveled across the country, walked out on the pool deck at Stanford, went up to his college coach and said, "I want to give it one more shot. I want my one moment in time that has been denied me." So they went to work.

Remember, Pablo had been away from competitive swimming for three years, and he would be twenty-seven years old if he made it to Barcelona. The times had gotten faster, the athletes had gotten younger, stronger and better, so he really had his work cut out. Pablo's training got underway and his times, little by little, came down.

Then on March 2, 1992, just six months after his return, Pablo made it back to the Olympic Trials in Indianapolis, not as a favorite but as a long shot. But wouldn't it be wonderful if Pablo could just make the Olympic team?

In the trial heats he swam well, not great, but good enough to qualify for the finals. Then that night as the gun sounded, his dad, Pedro, sitting in the stands on the far side of the pool held in his hands a photograph of Pablo's mother. With the picture moving in tandem, he followed Pablo down the pool and back, so that his mother, Blanca, could see him swim in the trials. And Pablo won . . . he won the trials. Pablo Morales was going to the Olympic Games.

Now it's a few weeks later, I'm on the pool deck in Barcelona and Pablo walks up. We had a nice chat and then he said, "Charlie, you won't recognize me tomorrow." I said, "Why not?" He answered, "Tonight is the night that we shave." (Swimmers shave all of their body hair so they can go faster through the water.)

Then a few days later it was time for the one-hundred-meter butterfly. In the trials Pablo swam well. He didn't swim great, but he swam well and he made the Olympic finals. What a wonderful comeback and wouldn't it just complete the story if Pablo could medal, if he could just finish in the top three.

That evening it was finally time for the finals of the men's one-hundred-meter butterfly. As Pablo stepped onto the blocks, I looked to the stands on the far side of the pool and there was his dad, Pedro, and in his hands was the photo of Pablo's mother, Blanca.

They fired the gun and Pablo, who's known for his strong start, takes it out. He has the early lead and the picture of his mother follows him down the pool. Pablo is leading at the turn. He starts back with fifty meters to go.

Pablo is still out in front with twenty-five meters to go, but Rafal Szukala of Poland and World Champion Anthony Nesty, with his great finish, are closing on him. He's still leading with ten meters to go fighting off their charge, but with five meters left Pablo starts to slip. It looks like he may lose but with one final effort Pablo stretches his arm and touches. I quickly look up at the scoreboard and it's flashing *Pablo Morales, Pablo Morales, Pablo Morales*. Pablo Morales has won the gold medal. He finally has his one moment in time, and you just know his mother Blanca is looking down and smiling her approval.

I saw him later that evening and facetiously I said, "Well, I guess that's the final chapter in the book of Pablo Morales?" He turned and looked at me with a little smile and said, "No, Charlie, that's the first chapter in the next book of Pablo Morales."

"The saga of Pablo Morales' risking failure,
risking looking foolish, then winning against all
odds . . . what a lesson he has for us.
So perhaps it's time for all of us, like Pablo,
to start the first chapter of our next book.
In my case, I took his advice and started the first
chapter, and I ended up with a whole book.
I hope you've enjoyed it!"

Contributors' Roster